# Contents

| | |
|---|---|
| Introduction | 4 |
| Part 1 | 10 |
| Chapter 1: Love and its mysteries | 11 |
| Chapter 2: What love feels like | 23 |
| Chapter 3: Set your feelings free | 36 |
| Chapter 4: The Stages of Love | 50 |
| Chapter 5: Finding "The One" | 62 |
| Part 2 | 76 |
| Chapter 6: How to Connect with Anyone | 77 |
| Chapter 7: Dating Survival Guide | 90 |
| Chapter 8: The Friend Zone | 107 |
| Chapter 9: How to Get Over Rejection and Thrive | 120 |
| Conclusion | 133 |

# The Love Formula

A Teen's Guide to Learn What True Love Feels Like, Get Over Breakups, and Ultimately Thrive in Love

**VENUS GALENA**

©Copyright 2022 - All rights reserved.

The content contained within this book may not be reproduced, duplicated or transmitted without direct written permission from the author or the publisher.

Under no circumstances will any blame or legal responsibility be held against the publisher, or author, for any damages, reparation, or monetary loss due to the information contained within this book, either directly or indirectly.

Legal Notice:

This book is copyright protected. It is only for personal use. You cannot amend, distribute, sell, use, quote or paraphrase any part, or the content within this book, without the consent of the author or publisher.

Disclaimer Notice:

Please note the information contained within this document is for educational and entertainment purposes only. All effort has been executed to present accurate, up to date, reliable, complete information. No warranties of any kind are declared or implied. Readers acknowledge that the author is not engaged in the rendering of legal, financial, medical or professional advice. The content within this book has been derived from various sources. Please consult a licensed professional before attempting any techniques outlined in this book.

By reading this document, the reader agrees that under no circumstances is the author responsible for any losses, direct or indirect, that are incurred as a result of the use of the information contained within this document, including, but not limited to, errors, omissions, or inaccuracies.

# Something for you

I wanted to share with you a special gift that I believe can make a positive impact in your life. It's a free self-love and self-improvement affirmation sheet that I've created to help you cultivate a more positive and empowering mindset.

The sheet is filled with uplifting affirmations that you can read and repeat to yourself every day. By focusing on these affirmations, you can train your mind to adopt a more confident and self-assured perspective, and make progress towards becoming the best version of yourself.

I truly believe that self-love and self-improvement are key to a fulfilling life, and I hope that this affirmation sheet can be a helpful tool in your journey. If you'd like to receive your free copy, please just let me know and I'll be happy to send it over.

Wishing you all the best,

*Venus Galena*

**Venus Galena**

# Introduction

True love doesn't need proof.
- **Toba Beta**

Love is everywhere around us, and yet it's so hard to find. I'm not talking about any type of love—I'm talking about genuine love. Love that's impossible to understand but brings us so much joy. It's with you through the trials of life, and never lets you go. It's love that's felt within the deepest crevices of your heart.

If you don't know what I'm talking about, you'll find out soon enough. Love comes in many forms. There isn't only one type of love, even though there's only one word in the English language for it. Love is complicated and confusing, especially when you don't know what it really feels like.

We can easily become trapped in false love when we ignore or miss all the red flags in front of our eyes. The hearts in our eyes stop us from seeing the truth, sometimes. Feelings overwhelm us and take control of our actions. The heart often overrules the brain, convincing us it's unnecessary to think; you must only feel. This isn't true.

I'm here to help you discover love and everything that comes along with it. Navigating the waters of love is a difficult river to cross, but once you give in to those waters and go with the flow, you can discover something beautiful. There will always be rocks in the way that try to block your path, but taking the first leap is exhilarating, even though it can be scary, too.

My teenage years were a time where I learned more about the world and what there is to experience. It was a time where I learned a lot about myself and my emotions. I had buckets of feelings that I couldn't explain. Suddenly, I noticed how handsome my best friend was. I became shy around him, whereas the year prior I didn't have a care in the world. I started fixing my hair and my dress to make sure I looked good for him at school. Every time I saw him, my heart felt like it was on fire. I tried to stay calm, but it was difficult to control my breathing. No one told me how to handle this. There was no one I could reach out and talk to; I had to figure it out on my own, and it was tough.

I made mistakes. I had embarrassing moments. We weren't meant to be, and yet his smile and terribly beautiful blue eyes haunted me for years. I could never get over him. Every time I thought I forgot about him, it would start all over again. I became obsessed with him, even though I knew it would never work out. Dwelling on him made it hard for me to enjoy the present moments I had. Thinking of the past made me depressed and heartbroken. I was sad, and I couldn't tell anyone why.

It took me a long time, but I began to focus on myself and what I loved. This eventually helped me heal and finally forget about this unrequited love. Now, I have the life of my dreams. I'm happy and in love with my wonderful husband and two daughters. I finally have the love I desired all along.

I wrote this book because I want to help those who struggle to understand what love really is. I want others to understand how to navigate love and life together. Many of my friends who have teenagers tell me how they've become depressed because of relationships, heartache, breakups, and loves that aren't meant to be. I've noticed that some of my own family members struggle to navigate love, too.

This book is for anyone who finds love confusing. This book is to help people, and especially teenagers, understand love. I want them to know what true love feels like, how to get through breakups, how to be happy in a relationship, and ultimately, how to thrive in love. Teenagers should feel confident and comfortable with love, and for that to happen it's important to understand your emotions. Teenage years are a time to experience many new things, and to experiment to find out things about yourself. This book will be a guide to help you make good choices within matters of love.

It's easy to get wrapped up in a relationship that's terrible for you, or to fall into the trap of 'real' love, which is far from true love. That's why this book will cover all the details of love that you'll find yourself trying to navigate. Instead of fearing love, you'll approach it with confidence. You'll not only learn to navigate it, but you'll also enjoy the journey.

Part one will be all about understanding love. Chapter one will help you learn what love actually is. Here, I'll guide you in understanding the different kinds of love. You'll understand more about the feelings you experience when you're in love, and you'll see why humans crave love and why love is healthy for us.

Chapter two will help you understand what the difference is between true love and false love. It will look at love vs lust, obsession, and infatuation. It'll help you discover whether the love you're experiencing now or have experienced before was true or not. When you're looking to begin a new relationship, you'll be equipped with the tools to recognize whether or not what you're feeling is genuine and whether that relationship is or isn't good for you.

Chapter three will help you understand your feelings. We'll discuss how important it is to let your feelings run free, and explore how you can express those feelings. It'll help you understand why it hurts when you lose the love you once had. I'll give you tips on how you can talk about your feelings and understand them better.

Chapter four will focus on the start of love. It'll describe how love blossoms, and how the start of a relationship should feel. It'll answer questions that are often difficult to understand, such as: Can love grow over time? Can love last forever? All your burning questions about the first stages of love will be answered.

In chapter five, we'll look at the concept of finding "The One" for you. Questions such as: Is it possible to find "The One"? Do we need to find "The One"? We'll take a look at what "The One" is and what we can do to find it, as well as focusing on the love we have for ourselves and how that will contribute to finding "The One."

Part two will give practical tips on how to succeed in love. Chapter six is all about how to connect with others. It will explain the different love languages and what you can do to figure out what your love language is. It'll also help you understand how to notice other people's love languages, along with some practical tips on how to communicate and connect with others.

Chapter seven is the ultimate dating survival guide. You'll get tips for your first date, your first kiss, and even on how to make the relationship official. They'll aid you in figuring out when someone is interested, how to invite someone out on a date, what you can do on the first date, what you can talk about during the date to create a deeper connection, and how to think of rejection differently. You'll also learn how to find the right moment to kiss, how to make it memorable, and how to make sure your partner understands your expectations.

Chapter eight will look at the dreaded friend zone and what to do about it. We'll discuss what you can do if you fall in love with a friend, and how to tell them. This chapter will help you out when you're stuck in the friend zone and teach you how to communicate your feelings clearly.

Chapter nine will look at breakups, heartache, and rejection. It's difficult to move past these things, but it is possible to do it and be happy in the present moment. We'll talk about why breakups hurt so much, and that it's okay to feel the way you do. I'll give you tips on how to get over a breakup, and how to find happiness again.

Exploring love can be daunting. By the end of this book, it should feel easier to navigate love and all of its ups and downs. Let's learn to understand love and all of its components together. If you'd like to explore the feelings you're experiencing and understand the love that you desire, join this rollercoaster of emotions with me. Relax, sit back, and enjoy the ride.

# Part 1

*Understanding Love*

# Chapter 1: Love and its mysteries

---

"Love is what makes the ride worthwhile."
- **Franklin P. Jones**

## What Love Means

This is a complicated statement with a complicated answer. People attach many meanings to the word 'love'. These four letters encompass a whirlwind of emotions. However, to discuss love, we have to break down its multiple meanings to understand how to identify this emotion. The simplest way to do that is by looking at the definitions that first pop up when we type out 'love' on our keyboards.

The first definition describes love as "an intense feeling of deep affection" (Oxford University Press, 1989). This explains that love isn't just a small, silly little thing. It's an intense feeling that often overwhelms us. When you feel that deep warmth within your heart and don't know why, it could be love. Love is felt within your inner being; it occurs deep within the soul.

Love is an affection that goes beyond surface level. Affection is a word to describe how you care for someone else. It shows just how fond you are of them, and it's completely natural if you feel this intense emotion deep within yourself.

The second definition describes love as "a great interest and pleasure in something" (Oxford University Press, 1989). This illustrates that we don't only feel love for people, but for things, too. Activities or places that you're passionate about can make you feel a certain way. We can feel love for anything we're fond of. If you're passionate about cars, for example, you can experience a love for them.

Love is much more than just "liking someone." Love is a two-way street. We should be able to both give and receive love, and it should be felt on both sides to be successful. Love means that you truly care about someone and their needs. You want them to be happy, and you want to be happy, too.

Love is earned over time. It takes time to realize that the love you have for each other is genuine. Love is about connecting more deeply and making an effort to understand each other. There's more to love than just attraction—love literally goes to the heart.

When you experience love, you experience a connection between two hearts. Love is growing and ever-changing. When you love someone, you trust them. Love is being present and listening to others. Because there are so many different traits of love, it's difficult to pinpoint one definition of it.

## The Philosophy Of Love

Looking at others' opinions on love can help us understand love in different ways. Because love is so complicated, there are many philosophers and writers who have tried to understand it, and as a result there have been countless poems, books, and short stories written about love and its intricacies.

Socrates was an Ancient Greek philosopher who believed that love is a quest for something good that you don't yet have. He believed that people search for love because it's a feeling they want, and that we all want what we don't have (Bhavan, n.d.). There is truth in this, because that feeling of love is indescribable and something that brings joy to our lives. In his words, "Give me beauty in the inward soul; may the outward and the inward be at one" (Socrates). He is therefore saying that when you're looking for love, you're looking for beauty both inside and out.

There's truth in all of his statements: We can only want love because we don't have it. Many believe that beauty and love go together. You don't know if you like a person until you speak to them, and the only way to approach them is by finding the courage to. When we feel attracted to someone, we likely have the urge to speak to them and find out more about them. Therefore, one notices the outer beauty of someone before their internal world is revealed.

Plato has a different take on love; this Athenian philosopher had many different ideas surrounding love. For Plato, love was about finding real beauty. The end goal wasn't love, but supreme beauty. His focus was on spiritual love. However, he recognizes that, at the start, love begins as a physical search. You first must recognize beauty in multiple bodies. This determines where you go to seek out beauty, or who you initially see as beautiful. After searching for physical beauty, you look deeper into the beauty of the soul. Then, after finding this beautiful soul, it in turn develops into moral beauty, the beauty of knowledge, the beauty of understanding, and ultimately, the beauty of the world (Ospino, 2021).

Okay, now hold on a moment—this has taken a very philosophical turn. Basically, what you can take from this is the realization of how deep love can actually go. But don't worry; romantic love doesn't have to be this complicated. Philosophers just like to think through things differently.

Paulo Coelho, a Brazilian novelist, has many definitions of love. However, one that stood out to me was "Love simply is." (Coelho, n.d.) These few words are so complicated, yet so simple. On the one hand, it explains that love is all around us. Love exists because it does. There's no rational explanation for it. Trying to figure out love in its entirety is impossible. Like Coelho says: "The wise are wise only because they love. The fools are fools only because they think they can understand love." (Coelho, n.d.) Coelho believes that love is only meant to be felt, not understood.

When looking at these different philosophers' and writers' opinions, we notice that everyone understands love differently. Because it's such an abstract concept, you can't put it in a museum to inspect it. And since every person is so different, it makes sense that everyone perceives it differently. Everyone has unique experiences with love and beauty. If love was reduced to just one meaning, it would be made insignificant. Throughout this book, you'll come to learn how to navigate love even if you don't understand the many different meanings of it.

## The Science Of Love

Without feeling, love would be meaningless. We've all felt that warm, fuzzy feeling in our stomachs. Some say it's butterflies, others have described it as a tingle, and some don't like the weird sensation it gives. But what is it actually? Why do we experience that strange feeling?

There are different chemicals released in your brain when you feel different emotions. When you're attracted to someone, you often experience feelings of lust. This is felt because of a rise in testosterone levels in men, and estrogen levels in women. When you feel attraction, you might experience your heart beating faster and your hands becoming sweaty. This is the noradrenaline chemical that gives you a boost of adrenaline. Phenylethylamine is the chemical that gives you that feeling of butterflies in your stomach, and norepinephrine gives you that warm fuzziness you feel. And of course, when you feel attraction your dopamine levels rise, making you feel good and happy.

When you start to create an attachment with your partner, the initial attraction chemicals get replaced by oxytocin and vasopressin, which is the chemical that makes you feel a bond and connection with your partner.

After that initial phase of first dates and nerves, the rush of feelings in the relationship fade into attachment. This is the stage where love really grows, and you form an intimate bond with each other.

Basically, all these chemicals make you feel happy when you're in love. They make you crave the feeling of the love you experience, since it's so adrenaline-filled.

## What Happens to Your Body?

Other than the obvious sweaty palms and raised heartbeat, falling in love can bring changes to your body. Some can be good, while others are bad.

Some of the good things are, for example, that love can boost your immune system. It can affect your health positively and can help you recover faster from illness, lower your blood pressure, and decrease your risk of heart disease. Along with this, when you see the one you love, you may experience less pain and your mood can receive a boost.

On the negative side, however, a new relationship can cause you lots of stress and anxiety. When you're around someone you like, it's difficult not to feel tense and stressed, because you want everything to work out well. Butterflies might fill your stomach, making you so anxious that you feel you're going to throw up. You may also lose your appetite and develop insomnia. This can have a noticeable effect on your sleeping and eating habits.

When we're in love, we often make silly mistakes or stupid decisions. We see our partner with hearts in our eyes. The hearts are too big to notice anything else, and can cloud our judgment and cause us to ignore the negative signs. We're so busy making it work that we overlook how bad the relationship might be for us.

## How Love Changes Your Brain

When you experience love, you experience different moods. Love gives you that giddy feeling. Just seeing or thinking about your partner makes you happy and excited. The chemicals in your brain make you feel relaxed and comfortable with your partner, especially after the initial honeymoon phase is over. It makes us gain trust in our partners and rely on them more.

Love can change your mind on many things, such as making sacrifices and having to compromise. It can help you accept these things more, and understand what your partner is expecting. When you crave more of your partner's love and you form a strong bond with them, it can create feelings of jealousy

within you. This isn't necessarily bad unless it gets out of hand.

Your mind can easily become obsessed with your partner. It can make you think constantly about them. However, something positive is the fact that feeling love helps you stress less. When you're secure in your relationship, it helps you feel less anxious and more happy.

Everyone's experience of love will be slightly different because of the different types of love we can experience.

## The Different Types Of Love

Different philosophers have divided love into three sections: The first type of love is called eros. This refers to sexual desire, the intense emotion of attraction and desire you can experience toward others (Mosely, n.d.). Plato believes that this love is necessary to find the ultimate beauty, as described earlier. This type of love is also ideal when it eventually develops into agape (which will be explained shortly).

The next type of love is called philia. This love is linked to friendship. It's the type of love that appreciates and cares for others and expects nothing in return. Being kind and fond of another person is what this type of love is about; it's a mutual understanding between two people (Mosely, n.d). Friends who you don't truly understand, or who you struggle to get along with, won't be linked to this love. You experience this love with your good friends. You have to be able to understand each other, be happy around each other, and be good to each other.

The last type of love is called agape. Agape is about an all-encompassing, perfect love. It's derived from the Christian type of love, which can be described as the love God has for humans (Mosely, n.d.). This love is deep and intense. It's love that doesn't change, even if that person has made mistakes. We should love each other as much as we love ourselves. Agape is about loving someone with everything in your heart, and putting your mind, soul, and strength into it. It's about forgiveness and making sacrifices. Agape combines eros and philia to create a perfect love that never changes or fails. This type of love never lets you down.

This book will focus on romantic love, also known as agape. We'll focus on what this love should look like and how we can recognize it.

## Why Do Humans Crave Love?

Humans crave love because they seek comfort band security. A sense of familiarity and trust is what you experience when you're with the one you love. Humans need to be surrounded by others—it's in our nature. We aren't isolated beings, and most people wouldn't survive for long without any human communication. When you have a companion, you're guaranteed to have someone by your side who fulfills your basic needs. Love is a basic need, according to Abraham Maslow. It's the missing piece that fits into the puzzle of life.

Since the beginning of time, humans have developed survival skills that taught us it's important to keep our population growing. We have the basic instincts of wanting to have children and wanting to care for those children. This is a natural part of our lives. From birth, we desire to experience human touch and love from others. A baby cries until they get picked up and held in their parents' arms. Without even knowing it, they're seeking human affection and attention.

Another reason humans crave love is the fact that it simply makes us feel good. The hormones produced when we're in love are the same pleasure hormones achieved from substances you can get addicted to, such as nicotine. We simply want to experience that feeling because it makes us feel good. It makes our problems melt away and makes us feel optimistic about life. Cuddling someone can make even our darkest days seem a little brighter.

We want to be acknowledged, and we want others to make us feel good. It's perfectly natural to want this in your life. Hearing kind words from others can really turn our day around. We crave love because it makes us feel wanted. When your partner shows they need you in their lives, it makes you feel important and worthy.

Humans can easily become insecure when they aren't supported or don't receive any kind words. When you experience love, you feel that someone needs you in their life, which is significant. This person wants you and chose you. You can't choose your family members, but you can choose your friends and partners. Therefore, it feels extra special when they choose to love you.

These reasons aren't necessarily your reasons for wanting to be loved. I'm not trying to force you to understand why you want love; All I want you to understand is that love is a natural thing for human beings, and that there are many reasons why it's healthy and beneficial for you.

Love can help us learn a lot about ourselves. It teaches us what we tolerate, what we don't see as acceptable, what we believe in, what we want to share with others, and so much more. Love is a way to drive yourself forward. It can give us the boost of energy we need to survive our day. It motivates us and helps us become more positive.

Falling in love and being loved are two very different things: Love is deep-rooted, whereas falling in love is surface level. It's important to figure out which is which. False love can come in many forms, and it's easy to be fooled by it. In this chapter, we've highlighted the following:

- love and its multiple meanings
- what philosophers think about love
- what happens to our body and mind when we're in love
- the different types of love
- why we crave love

Chapter two will break down love and compare it against the false love that you might fall for. It will give you the tools to recognize if what you're experiencing is genuine or just a phase in your life that will be easy to get over.

# Chapter 2: What love feels like

---

True love is supposed to make you into a better person and uplift you.
- **Emily Giffin**

# THE LOVE FORMULA

Unfortunately, genuine love is hard to come across. We often have to make mistakes before we find a love that's real. It's easy to believe that you've found it, only to realize later that it wasn't true love. False love puts on a disguise for you to fall for. It reveals itself only once the cloak is pulled off. When we're in love, we miss the many red flags that come up during the relationship. When that relationship is over and your eyes are finally open to seeing all the red flags, you might realize how shocking it was that you missed all the signs. But don't worry, we've all experienced this in some form or another.

There's a difference between experiencing love and experiencing lust, infatuation, and obsession. When you experience these feelings alone, it isn't truly love. There's more to love than attraction. As we move through each feeling, we'll discover why each of these individual emotions aren't love in its entirety and cannot ever be love.

24

## Love Vs Lust

Lust starts with physical attraction. It has nothing to do with emotional attachment; when you feel lust, you're only focusing on your physical desires. When you lust after someone, you like how they look and how they make you feel. A simple touch on the arm might make your heart jump inside your chest.

When you lust after someone, you're after the exciting feeling you experience when you see them, talk to them, touch them, or become intimate with them. It's all about sexual attraction. The focus is on the physical body and having a physical connection. Lust is something you can feel with or without love. For example, you might be sexually attracted to someone you don't know. This is experiencing lust without any love. When there is love involved, you might lust after your partner who you're already in a relationship with.

When you love someone, the focus is more on emotional attachment. Yes, you can experience lust in love, but love doesn't solely seek physical attraction and affection. It's about a mental, emotional, spiritual, and romantic connection. It's about deeply connecting with each other and understanding one another. Knowing where the boundaries are and how to respect them are all a part of love. This doesn't mean that you won't feel any sexual attraction in love—in fact, it's great to have physical attraction along with a deeper connection.

There are easy ways to recognize when you feel only lust toward someone, and when it's love. When you only think about someone sexually, for example, imagining how it would be to kiss and touch them, this is lust. Another example is if you don't care about their interests and don't care to have any meaningful conversation with them; you only want to be intimate with them. This is a sign that you're experiencing lust. If you're constantly daydreaming or fantasizing about this person, this is also a clear sign. Another indicator is if you don't want to have this person around you in your daily life, but only in intimate spaces.

Not all of these examples mean that you're strictly lusting after someone. Ask yourself questions and see if you're only after the physical attraction, or care about them more than that.

If you're in a relationship where your partner is mostly concerned with having a physical connection instead of an emotional one, you might have to rethink whether this person really wants a serious relationship or if they're just messing around with you. When two people understand the relationship in two different ways, it can easily lead to heartbreak. You might be more in love than they are, so it's important that you recognize lust vs love.

You can notice if someone is lusting after you by the following signs:

- They compliment your body and appearance a lot.
- They constantly want to do more than just kiss.
- They don't really want to talk about any deep topics.
- They don't want to talk about the future.

- When they see you, they immediately want to be physical and intimate.

Lust isn't necessarily a destructive emotion. In fact, it can be a healthy part of a relationship. However, pure lust is negative when you want love and a relationship based on emotional connection, when you mistake it for love, or when someone tricks you into believing that they love you while they're only lusting after you. Now that you know the difference, you can look out for the signs of lust.

## Love Vs Infatuation

Infatuation is also a feeling often mistaken for love. With infatuation, you experience powerful feelings of attraction toward someone. These feelings are so strong and overwhelming that you fixate only on the emotions you're experiencing. It's possible to feel infatuation toward someone who you don't know well and who fascinates you. When infatuated, you often make up dream scenarios in your head. You might picture yourself and this person together and create a happy fantasy world with them. When you're infatuated, you often ignore or overlook red flags because you've created this positive image in your mind of a person you can't change. You deem them as perfect in your mind when, in reality, they aren't.

This usually happens when you don't know a person well yet, but find them attractive. According to you, the brief conversations you've had were magical, and you've convinced yourself that you're going to spend the rest of your life with them. Having a crush on someone often leads to infatuation. This is very normal in the dating world.

The problem arises when infatuation gets mistaken for love. Because you experience such a powerful wave of emotions, it's often misleading, and these feelings can cause you to think that you've found true love. You become confident and say that you've finally found "The One" without taking anything else into consideration.

There are ways to realize that you're infatuated with a person. For instance, when you can't stop thinking and fantasizing about someone, you create high expectations of them in your mind, and when they don't reach them you either ignore it or feel disappointed. It becomes almost obsessive, and you form powerful feelings that come out of nowhere.

Infatuation is different to love because it's quick-paced. Love grows over time, and it's good when it takes time; infatuation happens quickly and can also pass very quickly. Infatuation is often surface level, whereas love goes deeper, into the soul.

Our emotions are all over the place, and it's difficult to calm down. We often become obsessed and jealous when we're infatuated with someone, and this is opposite to love, which is patient and trustworthy. Infatuation blows things out of proportion, making your attraction overwhelming. When infatuation occurs, you fall in love with the person you created in your head instead of the one in real life.

If you're infatuated, you're unsure if the other person is in love with you. It's very unpredictable. Infatuation turns your crush into an object you want; it's not really about the person's inner being. When you're infatuated, your expectations for the other person are very high, and they can't reach most of these expectations.

Infatuation makes you focus on only one thing, and the object of your infatuation feels like the most important person in the world to you. Love integrates gradually into your life, whereas infatuation makes you forget about your life. It makes you create a perfect world with a perfect partner and the perfect relationship. When you're in love, you realize that this perfect world isn't possible.

It's difficult to figure out whether or not you're infatuated, but you can try asking yourself how well you know this person. Are you making them up in your head, or do you really know them? Do you think they're perfect? Are you constantly thinking about them and nothing else? Take notice of these signs and see whether what you feel is love or only infatuation.

There's nothing wrong with feeling infatuation if it turns into something more. Infatuation can easily turn into love. The problem arises when you create a fantasy image in your mind and the person doesn't live up to these ideas, or when you can't move on with your life because you're so infatuated. This is why you have to understand the differences between when you're experiencing love and when you're experiencing infatuation.

## Love Vs Obsession

Obsession is, once again, very different from what love should look like. Obsession can be healthy in moderation, but some become so obsessed that it becomes harmful to others. Obsessive people have behaviors that can be the opposite of what love is supposed to be. When you're obsessive, you're possessive. You often want a person to belong only to you. Whenever they hang out with friends, you struggle to trust them and feel angry that they're not with you instead.

An obsessive person will want to see you as much as possible and constantly keep in touch with you. This can get so bad that they try to take your independent life away from you. Obsessive individuals believe that they are crucial in your life. They often give you ultimatums or force you to make decisions that are unfair. For example, if your partner asks you to choose between them or your family. You can't have both by your side; it's either one or the other. Obsessive people don't like to share you.

Obsession drives you crazy. It makes your emotions run wild, and makes you want to do wild things for a person. Obsessive individuals may even get to the point of stalking you. They want to know what you're doing every second of every day. They stalk your social media profiles and question any pictures you have of others who are close to you.

When you have an obsession with someone, it's difficult to form trust with them since you want to follow their every move. A person can't build trust with their partner if they can't do anything without their partner. If anything, their partner does is done without them, the obsessive person will become suspicious and will feel insecure. The obsessive person thinks more about themself than their partner, and they don't do nice and affectionate things for their partner. They only want their partner to do things for them.

Obsession often occurs because people feel insecure in their relationship, or they feel that they won't ever find a partner. Their anxiety worsens because of the fear that they won't ever find someone to love.

An obsessive relationship is fast paced. Since an obsessive person wants to give you a reason to stay in the relationship, they move fast. They'll constantly want to talk to you and can't live without sending you constant texts. Your approval is desperately needed, and they want to know whether you're in love and happy with how things are going. They'll do things to satisfy you just to feel secure. This shows just how much they place their own needs above those of others'.

When you're obsessed, you rarely want people to grow. You don't want them to move on or become independent. If they become independent enough, they might leave you and cause you heartache. When they want to make a big decision to change their life, you often won't support those decisions.

Of course, when you're in love, wanting to be close to each other and know each other's whereabouts is perfectly normal, but obsession turns the perfectly normal into something abnormal. It turns feelings of attraction into feelings of desperation.

When someone is obsessed, they easily overlook your achievements and focus on their own selfish desires. For example, if you got chosen to be head girl, you'd expect your partner to be happy for you. Instead, they would only fear that you'd fall in love with the head boy.

Obsession leads people to want to please you. They'll say

the things you want to hear instead of the things they believe. They might make you feel guilty when you want to do something they don't approve of, but they'll do this indirectly by using manipulation. If they don't want you to go on a holiday with friends, for instance, they could make you feel guilty by saying you've done so much for them and now suddenly you're deciding to disappear. This is a manipulation tactic they're using to get what they want.

When you're unhappy with what this person's been doing, they make empty promises. They promise to change and do anything for you, but they don't ever really change their behavior, only pretend to do so. This is because they don't feel like change is necessary. They make you feel like the relationship you have is the most important thing in the world, and nothing else in your life needs attention.

Obsession can easily lead to your partner becoming verbally or even physically abusive. When they don't get what they want, they'll do anything to get their way, no matter what stands to prevent it. They apologize quickly but fall back into their same habits. They don't want you to chase your dreams and try to shackle you down in the relationship.

It's extremely unhealthy if obsession leads to abuse. It can make you feel trapped and hopeless and can take a great toll on your mental health. We must look out for the signs of obsession and be sure to separate it from love. They're two very different concepts. Once you understand this, you can start to understand love.

## Am I In Love?

Now that you understand the differences between love, lust, infatuation, and obsession, it's time to ask yourself what you're feeling. Think of love you've experienced before, or love you may be experiencing now. Are there any differences in the love you've experienced? Was it really love, or was it one of the three concepts we discussed above? Ask yourself questions such as:

- Do you want to get to know your partner better?
- Do you want to spend a lot of time with them?
- Are you thinking about them a lot?
- Do you want to learn more about their lives?
- Are you excited by the idea of getting to see them and spend time with them?
- Do you feel happy and comfortable around them?
- Do you want them to know more about your life?

If you answered that you want to get to know them on a deeper level, then you are indeed after love. However, if you want nothing serious and are only attracted to them, this might be one of the other options. Think about it some more before moving forward.

## The One Question

This question will help you realize how much this person means to you. It will be the key to knowing if you're really in love and not mistaking it for another emotion. The question is:

- If you lost it all one day—your job, house, and all your money—but you had this one person with you, would you still be happy?

Let that sink in, and think about this question properly. If you answer it honestly, it reveals where you find yourself in your life and if this person is the one for you. This will tell you if you feel lust, infatuation, obsession, or love. The person you love should be the person you want to spend your time with, no matter what happens.

Now that we've questioned love and its false side, we can go on to understand how to express love. In this chapter, we've highlighted the following:

- The difference between true love and lust, infatuation, and obsession
- How to notice true love
- The questions to ask to find out if you're in love

In love, it's important to express your feelings. In chapter three, we'll see how vulnerability is important in love, but also how it opens us up to possibly experience heartbreak. We'll look at how people hide their feelings, and why they do it. This will help us understand what we can do to express ourselves. We need to set our feelings of love free to truly experience it. Let's explore why this is so important.

# Chapter 3: Set your feelings free

♡

---

Love is a serious mental disease.
- **Plato**

Many of us have a jumble of emotions inside us that we don't know what to do with. We might have a crush on someone but haven't talked to anyone about it. We bottle it all up inside because of the fear of humiliation or feeling vulnerable. Being in love is difficult to explain. It's hard to express what you're feeling, and why you're feeling what you are.

By expressing ourselves, we can figure out what we're really feeling and who those feelings are for. I've always felt better once I'm able to put my feelings into words. If you can set your feelings free, it can help you move forward and decide on what the next step is going to be. But it isn't as easy as it sounds; for some, expressing their feelings comes more naturally than it does for others.

## Why Do People Hide Their Feelings?

There could be multiple reasons why people don't enjoy showing their emotions. One of these could be heartbreak. Someone may have experienced heartbreak in their past and doesn't want to go through that pain again. Therefore, if they possibly develop feelings for someone, they hide it because they're scared of going through that heartbreak again. Instead of looking at the positive, such as the possibility that it could actually work out, they hide their feelings because they're focusing on the what-ifs.

Another reason that people might want to hide their feelings is that they've experienced humiliation and embarrassment after opening up. Maybe someone teased them when they were vulnerable, and they feel that if they were to open up, people would be mean and degrade them, making them feel worthless and upset.

People can also hide their emotions because they're used to it. They could be the type of person who prefers to bottle up their emotions because they feel like people don't want or need to hear what they're feeling, and that it's better left private. However, they often struggle to keep it all bottled up, which can lead to an outburst of emotions if they don't watch out.

Others may hide their feelings because they simply think no one cares. They're insecure and feel like no one would listen if they talked about them. This could be because in previous situations where they wanted to share their emotions others ignored or spoke over them. They could have been building the moment up in their heads about having a serious conversation and talking about their feelings only to be ignored or shrugged off. This could make them feel that they aren't wanted or that no one cares to hear what they have to say.

They might also fear that talking about it could end up making them feel worse about the situation. When an issue is put into words it becomes a reality, and this might make them feel that their feelings aren't valid or that they shouldn't be having them at all.

Another reason is that they don't want to hurt anyone with their words. Maybe they dislike what someone is doing, and this has been making them feel upset. So, they hide their opinions because they don't want to hurt said person or cause emotional pain. They put an emotional wall up that's difficult to break, shutting down everyone who they care about or cares about them.

They could also hide their feelings because they don't want to change their relationship with you. For example, let's say you fall in love with your best friend. You've known each other for years and have a great relationship. But now, you're developing romantic feelings. You don't want to reveal these feelings in fear of damaging the good relationship you already have. Basically, you don't want to make things awkward and change the relationship dynamic. You just want everything to stay the same as it is between you only with romance attached, but you're scared that it might change everything.

There are many reasons for hiding your feelings. There are several more that haven't been listed here, but your reason for hiding your feelings might be related to some of these examples. One of the biggest reasons is that love hurts—and hurting doesn't feel good.

## Why Love Hurts

Love hurts because it's intense. It hurts because it resonates on a deeper level and is attached to your emotions. When you're hurt emotionally, it physically hurts you, too. Social pain makes us hurt physically because it's connected to everything; it's an emotional reaction to things such as heartbreak, loneliness, death, big changes in your life, and feeling disconnected. When these situations occur in your life, you feel physical pain because of your powerful emotions. Therefore, it hurts when you have true feelings and this thing you thought was love has been taken away from you.

This is usually a big change in your life and affects you emotionally since you had someone that meant a lot to you or who was a big part of your life. When something like this is whisked away from you suddenly, life can feel totally different, which can lead to physical pain.

But there's a reason you suddenly feel physical pain after you lose a love: When you're in love, your body releases chemicals that make you feel excited and happy. When you're away from this person or will no longer be seeing them anymore because of a breakup, it causes a chemical crash, leading you to feel sad and upset. This is the equivalent of a sugar crash. After you have loads of sugar, you feel energetic, but hours later you might feel exhausted and lazy. This is simply because your blood sugar levels have crashed, and now your body is experiencing the aftermath of the many sweets you ate. Something similar happens when you're away from the one you love. All the chemicals that were released when you were with your partner return to normal, and you can physically feel the pain when you aren't with them.

Love hurts when you have high expectations, and your needs aren't met. For example, when you love someone, you probably think they're the perfect one for you. You're in love with everything about them until you discover there are flaws you don't like about them. This disappointment can physically hurt you and cause you distress.

Thinking about the future can also cause you physical pain. It's very difficult to only focus on the present when you're in a relationship. After all, many people want to find the one they'll marry and spend the rest of their life with, but this can cause stress and anxiety. Uncertainty creeps in, and all the what-ifs float through our minds. We become anxious about whether this person is really the one, and it hurts to be uncertain about the future. We wonder whether it'll be just another failed relationship, and what will happen if it is.

We worry whether the relationship is going too fast or too slow and what to do about it. We worry about big milestones, such as when we'll meet the parents and what they'll think of us, will they love us back, will we move in together, and much more. The future is uncertain, and that's scary.

The baggage we bring into a relationship is from past hurt. This makes it more difficult to love in the present moment because we constantly think about what happened before and if it'll happen again. It's difficult to move past previous pain because we remember how bad it felt. It causes pain to even think about the past pain we've experienced because we don't want the same thing to happen in the present.

When there's conflict, love hurts. You don't want to hurt your partner, but a disagreement is inevitable, and causes a lot of pain. When you hurt someone, it causes that person and yourself a lot of pain. It can be very difficult, and the expectations of love can become overwhelming, causing a lot of pain.

The longer you experience love, the more it'll hurt when it goes away, especially if it was love and not lust, infatuation, or obsession. And that's the difficult thing about love—it's a tricky road to follow. When things go well, they go really well, but when they go wrong, they cause heartbreak and pain. I think that love is an important gamble to make, because in the long-term it can bring you ecstatic joy and a life you've always wanted. To experience love, you should first be able to express it.

Set your feelings free and be open to embracing it. But why is that so important?

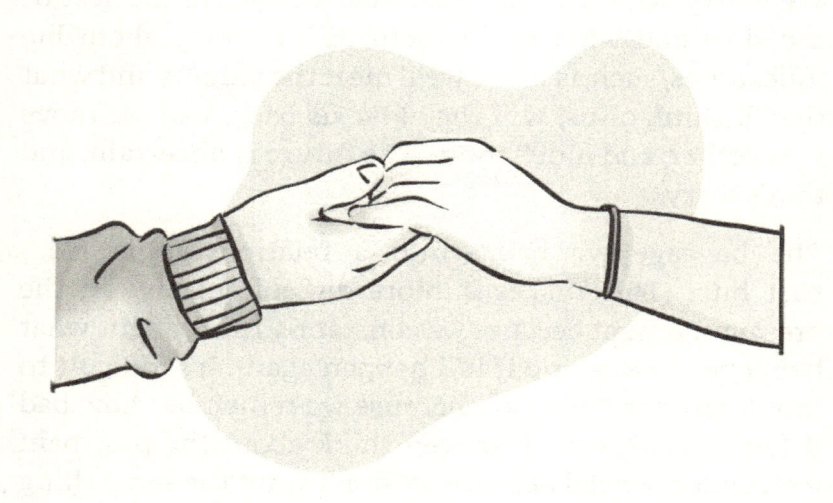

## The Importance Of Expressing Your Feelings

It's important to express your feelings, because if you don't, it can affect you negatively. When you don't express your feelings, it can make you feel worse than you already are. Letting it all out helps you to blow off some steam. When you don't express your feelings, it can frustrate important people around you. This might put a strain on a relationship if they know something is wrong, but you don't want to tell them what's going on. It can cause more difficulties in your relationships and more pain in your life.

When you can't express your feelings, you can't communicate what you're feeling. And, as we all know, communication is important in any relationship. To be open and honest is necessary for any relationship to thrive. The more you keep your feelings in, the longer you'll dwell on them. When you don't let it go, the anger and sadness only continue to rise until an outburst is inevitable. Or, if an outburst doesn't happen, those feelings will only make you feel bad inside.

Expressing your feelings is human. It isn't something we should be afraid of. We're born to think and feel, so there's nothing wrong with expressing those things. Feelings are confusing, and if just one other person can relate to what we're going through, it already makes us feel better.

There are multiple benefits to expressing our feelings. When we verbalize the issues we're facing, it's easier to think clearly and see things differently. If something is stuck in your head, it's hard to understand it from an outside perspective, but when you explain to others how you're feeling about it, they might see it from a different angle that could help you.

When we speak about our emotions it makes them seem less significant, and that's usually a good thing. For example, when you're furious that you stubbed your toe and have had a bad day because everything seems to be going wrong, you can express these feelings. When you say it out loud, you're able to realize that it's silly to get angry over a stubbed toe and let it ruin your day.

When you can express your emotions, you understand yourself and where you're coming from a bit more. It's important to understand yourself, and it helps you to practice self-love and care. If you chastise yourself in your head and think badly about yourself, you can never love others the way you should.

Expressing your emotions is a way to get rid of the stress and anxiety you're facing. This doesn't mean that it totally takes it away, but that it can calm you down. When your emotions are out of your head, you feel lighter and more in control of them. It makes you build resilience against the feelings you're facing and helps you to see that you can get through many things in life.

Once these emotions are out, it can help turn your feelings into something more positive. You'll be more confident once you're in tune with your emotions and when you aren't ashamed of speaking to them.

Expressing your feelings has many positive benefits to your well-being, and negative ones when you don't. However, each person is different, and what might work for one might not work for another. It's never bad to try something new. If you're not used to expressing your feelings, test it out and see how you feel afterwards. There's one way to do this in particular that proves to be most effective.

## The Best Way To Do It

Expressing your emotions shouldn't be an angry outburst where screaming is involved. It should be done in a calm and logical way. One way you can do this is to think things over in your mind before saying them out loud. Think about the exact emotion you're feeling, and what you think caused it. Accept the feelings that you have, even though you don't want to have them. If you ignore or deny them, they'll just become worse and hurt you more. Instead of screaming at someone because they made you angry, try to understand your emotions first.

With that being said, don't hide any of your emotions. Be honest and open and allow yourself to feel vulnerable. When you hide your feelings, you can't connect with yourself or others. You can share your feelings, either positive or negative, calmly. You don't have to be rude or express them with anger and hatred. Feel what you're feeling and express it clearly.

If you don't understand your emotions clearly, talk through it. It's okay to say, "I don't know what I'm feeling," or "I don't understand it right now, just give me time." This is normal. Feelings can be a mess inside your head, and to discern what made you feel that way is tricky.

If you want to share your feelings, the best way to do it is to talk to someone you trust. It must be to someone who makes you feel valid. It doesn't help you share your feelings with someone who will laugh at them and think you're being ridiculous. Stick to your close friends and family members if you're opening up for the first time. Being vulnerable is hard and scary, and no one wants to feel humiliated.

If you feel you have no one to talk to, or that you don't have a person like this, you can reach out to a therapist or someone with an unbiased opinion. This will help you feel more comfortable expressing your emotions. And if you get used to talking to someone you don't know and who wants to help you, maybe you can muster up the courage to talk about your feelings to someone you know and care about.

When you have an argument and you want to express your feelings, try to understand where the other person is coming from first. Others' emotions often make us feel angry or hurt, but if you take a closer look at them, you might understand why that person is expressing themselves in the way that they are. Try to understand through practicing empathy. However, make sure you're still expressing your emotions even if others don't understand yours very well. Then it's their turn to express empathy and understanding. It must go both ways.

When we have emotions, we often try to distract ourselves with

other things to shove them to the side. This isn't healthy, as the feelings are still there. The best way to understand your emotions is to get rid of all your distractions and think about it clearly in your mind. Go sit somewhere quiet and write your thoughts down. This will often help to understand them more.

If you're holding emotions back because you don't want them there or you feel they're not valid, it's time to forgive yourself and others. Tell yourself that it's okay to feel what you're feeling. If you're angry with someone else, try to forgive them and let those emotions go. Don't only forgive yourself, but also accept what you're feeling. Accept what happened and what caused your emotions and learn to let go of it by slowly forgiving yourself for it.

Sometimes we struggle to express our feelings because we feel like we don't deserve to be happy. But everyone is allowed to be happy, no matter what's happened to you in your past. You deserve to express your feelings and be happy in all aspects of your life.

With setting your emotions free, there's always a risk. However, the reward is great, too. Be open to expressing your feelings and be optimistic about the benefits it can bring to your life. Most people are very open to listening to your feelings and will be empathetic and more than happy to be there for you. Taking the leap is the best option to feel fulfilled.

Remember that feeling emotion is valid and normal. Every human being experiences it in their daily life. It's something that's unique to you, and that's exciting. Exploring your inner being is an interesting endeavor that takes a long time to understand, but setting your feelings free can help to untangle it more.

Don't be too harsh to yourself. If you're hard on yourself you stand the chance of only making it worse and preventing yourself from loving the way you should.

Now that we understand how to express our emotions, we can go deeper into the specific emotion we're focusing on, which is love. In this chapter, we've highlighted the following:

- Why people often hide their real emotions
- Why love hurts
- Why it's important to express your emotions
- How to express your emotions clearly

VENUS GALENA

In chapter four, we'll look at how love begins and grows, and whether love can actually last forever. The stages of love are important to understand when wanting to jump into understanding the world of love.

# Chapter 4: The Stages of Love

♡

---

There is no remedy for love but to love more.
   **- Thoreau**

There are multiple stages of love. Many may feel like their love is perfect from the start, but it isn't really. There are several things' couples have to go through before they can be certain they've found the love they need and want. But before we fast-track to deep growing love, we must first look at how it all starts. When you understand the stages of love, you'll quickly recognize what love isn't.

## How Love Begins

### Stage One: Passion

Stage one is the most exciting stage of love. It's where everything seems perfect; everything is overwhelming and joyous and new and wonderful. It's the time where we don't think, but feel. We enjoy the pleasures of the hormones our bodies release and are happy that this new relationship has started. It's a disruption in our lives, but it's a good disruption, so long as you don't sacrifice everything in your life just for this person. You must still be able to live your own life as well as enjoy the time you have with your partner.

When a relationship starts, everything is uncertain. You're still unsure about their emotions, how they feel about you, what they like about you and what they don't, and if you're doing the right things or not. At the moment, you're just enjoying each other and trying not to think about anything that could be wrong with this person. You still see them as the perfect one for you, and that's a good thing. Every relationship should start off like this.

You should be excited to see each other, be close together, spend lots of time with each other, and experience falling in love together. The first stage is important, because it shows that the attraction is there and that it can turn into something more.

With hearts in your eyes, you can happily be with each other. Every single moment with them is exciting. Your heart feels warm when you're in their arms, and everything they say makes your heart flutter.

You feel an intense attraction for each other, and every look you share and thing you do is passionate. It all seems to work out well at the start. It's a feeling of euphoria and bliss, and you're constantly thinking about this person both when you're with them and when they're not around.

However, the beginning stages can also bring you anxiety. Fitting a new relationship along with all the other duties in your life is difficult, at first. You don't know what you should sacrifice, or if you should sacrifice anything at all. It can cause you stress when you have less time to do the things you enjoy or need to do.

You can feel tired at the beginning stages of love, simply because you're dealing with a lot of hormones at once, or you could lose sleep because you keep thinking about this person and the excitement makes it difficult for you to sleep. You may stay up later than you usually do just for them.

This wild and scary journey is all part of the first steps of a new relationship.

**Stage Two: Settling In**

Now that the whirlwind of crazy emotions is over, it's time to settle down. This doesn't mean the relationship should be any less exciting—it just means that you're now at that stage where you're more comfortable with each other. You understand each other better and your hormones are settling down.

This is the time where you talk about more serious things, such as what you envision for the future, how the relationship is going to move forward, and what the next big step is. You plan your future together and discuss your opinions on different topics: Do you like dogs? Would you want a pet one day? Where do you see yourself living? What job do you want in the future? How many kids do you want? And so on and so forth.

You're thinking of the reality of your relationship now, and what the possibilities could look like. It makes you excited about the future when you can picture them in your life. You understand more about them and gain a deeper look into their soul (if it was possible to look into one). You understand each other a lot better and appreciate each other for who you are.

## Stage Three: Reality

This is the stage where you realize your partner isn't perfect. There's no such thing as someone who's perfect. We were made to be imperfect; there's simply no way we can do everything in life perfectly. You realize that you and your partner disagree on some things or see certain aspects of life differently. This is the time where arguments begin, and where you realize that you and your partner have many differences.

At this stage, your partner makes mistakes that you're disappointed in, and they might feel disappointed, too. It's the stage where you have to make tough decisions and communicate clearly to move forward. Here, you must handle the differences and come up with solutions to improve the relationship and come to an agreement.

The hearts in your eyes are gone as you start to see the bad things about your partner. You notice the baggage, the annoying habits, and the opinions you don't agree with. This is the most difficult stage of a romantic relationship. If you don't get past this, you're most likely to break up. You might think the baggage is too much or their opinions too different, and this is where it all ends. Reality sets in, and it's not always fun to look at.

When you go through this stage, it doesn't mean that you're failing at your relationship and love in general. It's normal and a part of every relationship. Unfortunately, not everything is sunshine and rainbows, even when we hope it is.

In this stage, you have to make big decisions. Do you still want this relationship to continue? Are they really the person for you? Is it worth pushing past these difficulties? Do you still love them, even with their flaws and mistakes? If you believe they're worth fighting for, then it's best to push forward. Otherwise, you can end the relationship and start all over again. It all depends on how you feel and what you think is best for you.

## Stage Four: Deep Love

Pushing past the third stage of love is very rewarding. When you accept your partner for who they are, you develop a deeper love and understanding for each other. Here, you have learned to forgive each other and work past the differences and arguments you once had. The differences aren't necessarily gone, but you've found a way to work through them together and work as a team instead of separately.

In this stage, you've both realized that love is more than the butterflies you felt at the start. This is the stage where you choose them. You choose to move past the difficult times and make a commitment to them.

This is where your love grows deep. It's like a tree: The roots are now deeply cemented, and the tree can only grow bigger from here. You've experienced highs and lows in your relationship and have faced hardship, and you've now entered the stage where you're fully comfortable with each other and accept the imperfections. Of course, there might still be some bumps in the road, but you'll now be able to handle them better and communicate well.

This love is a love that loves the mind, body, and soul. You're at that stage where you choose to love everything about your partner.

**Stage Five: Working in Harmony**

At this stage, you know each other so well that you can work really well together. You fill in each other's flaws and work together as one. You are literally each other's puzzle pieces. The deep integration of your world and theirs makes it impossible to imagine a world without them. Life wouldn't be good without them. This is where a couple works very well together, and it's not because they've always had a perfect relationship, but they've worked together to create the perfect relationship.

Many, however, don't get to experience all these stages of love because they don't make it past the third and most difficult stage of a relationship. It's difficult to do, and a couple isn't always meant to get past it. Only the ones who are truly meant for each other get past this stage.

When you've found your partner for life, it's easier to work past the difficulties in life. When you realize that there are better days after the hardships, it helps to tackle these hard times.

## Can Love Grow Over Time?

The short answer is yes, time makes love grow. There are various stages of love that we have to understand when we want to experience love. Love doesn't just come quickly; it's a process. It's the one thing that improves over time. Love becoming old is a good thing.

However, love can either grow, or it can die out. Love that dies out was never genuine love, because true love cannot fail. The longer love grows, the stronger the relationship becomes. When love dies out, it fades away, and you realize that the flaws and baggage of the person were too much to handle. Some relationships are just not meant to last.

Love that grows is a beautiful and precious thing. It's rare, and if you find it, you should do your best to keep it. Love that grows is love that accepts all flaws and works together to live in happiness and harmony.

Unfortunately, many people experience love that dies out. You may have thought you had true love, but the butterflies die out and so does the relationship. The only thing keeping the relationship afloat was the excitement of the first stage of love, but after that, the love became boring, tedious, and hard work that wasn't worth it. This could be because you didn't work on building up the foundation of the relationship, which are things like communication, trust, loyalty, and teamwork.

## THE LOVE FORMULA

The relationship may have been full of communication gaps and misunderstandings, and you were simply going through the motions with this person. This can lead to love fading out.

When love grows, the foundation firmly stays in place, and you know where you stand with each other. Yes, you experience difficulties and arguments sometimes, but real love isn't boring. It's the small things that matter most. When you love, even the small moments can make you smile and change your mood. Love that grows brings about happiness to a couple. They're satisfied with how they're living their life and want to continue this growth.

With love that dies out, the two parties weren't putting any effort into making the relationship grow or salvaging it. They feel like all hope is lost, and that there's nothing they can do about it. Love that grows keeps working on the relationship, even through difficult circumstances.

The only way for love to grow is for it to be a two-way street. When one gives their all but receives nothing in return, it can be very exhausting and hard on the person. For love to work, you must work together. One person shouldn't be putting more effort in than the other. It should be equal.

It all depends on whether you want to make it work with the person or if you feel like the relationship won't work and won't ever change for the better. It's all up to your circumstances. If your love grows over time and you develop deeper feelings for each other, you're on the right track. If you feel that love has grown boring and everything irritates you about your partner, it might be time to rethink your relationship and what to do about it.

## Can Love Last Forever?

This is a hard question to answer, and I don't think anyone has the definite answer. We've all heard about couples that have been together their whole lives. It's their 55th wedding anniversary, and you think to yourself, "How can they put up with each other for so long? Do they really still love each other?"

The answer is that they've grown to understand each other. They might not always like each other, but that love and mutual bond will always be there. There are, of course, married couples who no longer feel love for each other anymore, but there are also those rare instances where you see couples that last forever. I believe that true love can last forever. Couples that last truly love each other fully. They continue to put effort in to make it work.

But love doesn't have to last forever. Just because your

love for someone didn't last doesn't mean it wasn't a happy stage in your life. Every failed relationship has meaning in it. I don't think you can call a relationship that ended one that failed. Feeling love for someone is already a gift, and every moment should be cherished. Yes, it was a stage of your life and it's gone now, but it was a necessary stage that was brilliant and heartbreaking at the same time. Not all past relationships were bad ones. Relationships can teach you many lessons and help you to realize what you want in life.

At each stage of your life, you've had to learn from the relationships you had. Not all were love, but each one makes you more certain of what you really want and what you believe love to be.

Love that lasts a lifetime can still be romantic. Instead of it being obsessive and a rollercoaster of emotions, it can be calming and have an overwhelming joy attached to it.

Love for family and friends can last forever. That's still love, even though it isn't romantic. It can be the same for romantic love, and for that to happen you have to find the one that you'd want to spend the rest of your life with.

Just because your love didn't last forever doesn't mean it was completely terrible. It might not have been the true love you were after, but there are always good times among the bad ones. So, the question is as complicated as the answer. Every person's love for another is unique.

It's all about feelings and emotions. Maybe you feel like this love will last forever, even if you go your separate ways. We can never have a definite answer because there's no science that can explain all of our abstract emotions.

That's what makes love so unique.

In this chapter, we've highlighted the following:

- the cycle of love and each different stage of love
- how love grows over time
- if love can last forever

By looking at the different stages of love, we can take it into consideration and realize how love should be. We need to realize that we have to get through the difficult times to experience the best ones. And once this happens, our love can grow even more over time. When we find the one, the love we share with that person can last forever.

Love has more stages than you realize: It starts out passionate with millions of butterflies. Then the butterflies settle in your tummy. After the butterflies settle, hard times are inevitable, but this mustn't make us lose hope. After we overcome these obstacles, a deep form of love grows, which leads us to eventually working together in harmony. This love of ours then grows and can lead to a long-lasting and wonderful lifetime of love. In chapter five, we'll figure out whether we can find "The One" and if there really is someone like this out there for us.

# Chapter 5: Finding "The One"

You must love yourself internally to glow externally.
- **Hannah Bronfman**

Is there a 'One'? Society has always emphasized that we must find "The One." The partner that will never leave your side. The fairytale happily ever after, the Disney movie wedding. We have this idea in our heads of the person who we think is "The One" and yet we can't seem to find them. You've been looking all over, but this person isn't easy to find.

But do we actually need to find "The One"? Do we need to set out on an adventure that might result in nothing? Is there a perfect person out there for us who's our soulmate and our happily ever after? And who exactly is "The One"? Billions of people live on this planet. How can we assume that "The One" lives in the same country as us, let alone the same town? Are we fooling ourselves with the concept of "The One?" Does everyone have an ideal mate in this world, or are we all just kidding ourselves? Who is this mystery 'One'?

These were all questions that once floated around in my mind until I realized who "The One" for me actually was. Is this a journey that we all have to go on? Let's find out whether you've already found "The One," or if you should still be searching.

## Do We Need To Find It?

Finding "The One" sounds like an impossible task. Do we really want to put in all the effort just to find someone we think is supposed to be with us forever? Maybe we like being alone and don't feel like we need anyone around us. "The One" sounds more like a pain in the butt to us. We would rather settle than to put in effort to find a person who might not even exist.

But what if I told you that there might not even be a 'One'? What if it doesn't exist? Society has constructed "The One" in our heads and made us believe that we all have to settle down with "The One." That when you're dating someone other than the person who's meant for you, you just delay the two people who are meant for each other from meeting. It feels cruel, like you're taking away love from someone else. But this isn't true. This is only a societal concept. Some people don't find "The One," and others are just happy in the current moment, which is good too.

If you obsess over finding "The One," you might not notice the happiness in your life already. Someone might be a good match for you, but because there's one slight thing that's in the way of them being "The One," you avoid the happiness you could have had. The images we create in our heads are often idealized and unreal. If you have these high expectations, you'll never find happiness.

You can be happy without "The One." If you constantly search for it and feel disappointed, you'll miss all the beautiful things in your life. Instead of waiting around or desperately trying to find "The One," focus on the good things already in your life. If you don't obsess over it, "The One" might come without you realizing it.

Also, "The One" could be right in front of you, and you'll only realize it later on. You might miss the amazing people in your life while you're looking for an idealized version of this person.

You can have one image in your head about the perfect person for you and it might end up being totally different. When we get stuck with the idea in our minds about the person we want, it can make us miss the people that truly need to be in our lives; just because he doesn't have curly hair and blue eyes like your dream guy doesn't mean that he isn't the one for you. We need to get rid of the obsessive image in our minds and be open to other possibilities. You never know, they might make you happier than you ever thought they could.

And if this idealized image in your mind is your idea of love, you're being misguided. Like I said, our minds create false fantasy worlds that aren't possible in real life. If we don't watch out, we can get caught up in this fictional world and have a false idea of what love is—the perfect person, life, and world.

"The One" is different for everyone. There isn't a generalized list of traits that everyone will fall in love with. There's no ideal person with ideal qualities in an ideal world. For some, "The One" can be someone who has the opposite qualities to what they have, and for others, "The One" is very similar to themselves. Creating one ideal image in your mind is a dangerous way of looking at love and can let you down easily.

As soon as someone moves away from the idea you have about your soulmate, they don't feel like "The One" anymore. This can lead to you being so unrealistically picky that you can't find any happiness at all.

Therefore, I don't think we need to fixate on finding "The One." If you're always desperately looking for it or have an unchangeable image in your head, you'll never find it. Love comes to those who aren't looking. Love has no rules. It can come unexpectedly, throwing you straight into the deep end. It can come when you least want it, but most need it. The goal should be to be happy, and if we aren't, to find happiness. Do we need to find "The One"? If finding it means finding happiness for you, then the answer is yes. If you already have happiness but feel like you don't have "The One," then it's no. It all depends on us as people.

## How Do We Attract It?

We attract "The One" by being ourselves. "The One" is a reflection of what we need in our lives. Our partner is there to live our lives happily with us. The relationship should be an integration into your life, not a separation from your life. It's not that hard finding "The One" if you stay true to yourself. If you're constantly searching for someone, it might be time to take a step back and enjoy your single life first. When you desperately search for something, you might choose the first person that comes your way, and this might not be good for you.

Being yourself will attract the right partner. If you can fully be yourself, the right person will love you for it. They won't want to change you or turn you into someone you're not. There's nothing special or out-of-the-ordinary you should be doing. The right person for you will love all your flaws, qualities, insecurities, and quirks. They'll be happy with everything you are. If they aren't happy with who you are, they might not be the one for you, or they're stuck in a fantasy idealized world of what "The One" looks like.

Don't hide yourself from others. Of course, when you first meet someone, you don't immediately tell them your entire life story, and that doesn't mean you're hiding anything. It just means you don't know this person well yet, and they don't know you. Start slow and learn more about each other as time goes on.

When you don't hide your true self, it means that you are who you say you are from the start. You're honest about what you like and dislike. You don't conform when they disagree with you (For example, if they hate the color orange and you don't, don't suddenly tell them that you hate orange, too.) The more lies you tell, the easier it'll be to expose those lies. Avoid lying and stay true to what you think and feel.

You need to be happy with yourself before you can be happy with others. Find out what type of person you are. When you get confronted by things that you aren't, stand strong and back up your opinions. This doesn't mean that you should be mean to others who don't share what you believe in, it just means you should be self-assured. Being confident is a good quality, and it attracts others.

Being yourself means doing so in every aspect of your life: on social media, in your work life, school life, and everywhere you go. We must trust that the right one will come in their own time. Desperation doesn't help, and, in fact, repels people away. Know that you are good enough to have someone in your life.

But who is "The One"? How can we find "The One" if we don't even know who they are? How do we know what we're looking for?

## Self-Love

Self-love is very important for love in general. Loving ourselves can make us ready for loving others. Once we have a good understanding of ourselves, we can figure out how to properly love others. When we love ourselves, it means we take care of ourselves and ensure we're in a good mental, emotional, and physical state. It becomes easier to tackle each day of lives with optimism and positivity.

If we don't love ourselves, it can place a strain in our lives, making each day harder. Sometimes we think a partner can fix this for us, when in reality a partner isn't supposed to fix your life; they're supposed to enhance it.

Self-love can benefit us in multiple ways by relieving stress, creating healthier habits, boosting confidence, boosting productivity, and much more. But how does it affect our relationships? Is self-love necessary in a relationship?

## Can You Love Another Without Loving Yourself?

I personally believe that you can love another person without loving yourself, however, you won't be able to properly appreciate their love or love fully if you don't love yourself first.

What I mean by this is that love goes both ways. You should both give love and accept love to ultimately experience it. When we don't love ourselves, we don't want to hear or accept any compliments we receive. People get upset when their compliments get rejected. They feel like they can't give you the love they want to give. When you constantly reject compliments, you're not seeing the significance of them, and this makes you ignore the love you're receiving. This could make others feel like it's difficult to love you, simply because you can't receive love. Showering each other with love is part of a relationship.

However, it is difficult to love yourself sometimes. It isn't something that's set in stone. Sometimes you can love yourself and other times hate yourself or your actions. Each day is a learning experience. Each day we learn how to grow our own love for ourselves. This means that you don't have to love yourself every day, but you do have to make sure you don't hate yourself. You must learn to be kind to yourself.

When you love someone, you don't have to be a different person, and if you are, it isn't a healthy relationship. You only have to be yourself and love yourself. Others will see and appreciate that, and the right one will come along eventually.

Therefore, you don't always have to love yourself, but making time to practice self-love and self-care is necessary when seeking a relationship. If self-love is missing, you'll be insecure and will likely struggle to receive love. When you love yourself, you can understand the love that you're receiving and can accept and be grateful for it.

## You Are "The One"

Surprise! All along, you have been "The One." The greatest kind of love is loving yourself. We can't love anyone else if we don't love ourselves. Self-love is very important in order to discover happiness and joy. You shouldn't search for a partner to find joy, but must find it within yourself. We live with ourselves every day, so the love we have for ourselves is the most important. You can't get away from or take a break from yourself—you're always there, and therefore you need to learn to live with yourself in harmony. The one you're looking for should be you first and foremost.

When you look for a partner, you're looking for someone who you can work well with. Someone who has qualities that compliment yours, and can inspire you to work on your flaws. Someone who can fill in the gaps you're struggling with. This doesn't mean that you're looking for someone to fix your flaws, but rather someone who encourages you to work on them and let you know it's okay to have them. To find that, you need to understand yourself and how your mind works. You must discover what attributes you do and don't have.

## How to Love Yourself

Now that you know you're the one you have to love first before you look for love elsewhere, you must figure out how you can build that love for yourself, and I'll help you do that. How can you possibly love every part of you? All the flaws, attributes, mannerisms, quirks, and more?

Loving yourself first means understanding yourself. Think of what your biggest strengths and weaknesses are, what you like and dislike, what you'd like to work on as a person, and what you love about yourself most. When you think of these things, you understand yourself more and learn to love each part of you. It may be a slow process, but when you accept your flaws, you can work on them to become a better person.

When you understand what your strengths are, you can use them to your advantage. This will give you a confidence boost and will help you see what you're capable of.

When you make mistakes, it's important not to be too hard on yourself. Everyone makes mistakes, and it's all part of being human. Loving yourself means accepting all parts of you, even the mistakes you make. It's difficult to do, and you can give yourself time to work through it, but you have to forgive yourself just as you forgive others.

Every person is different, and some people just don't understand each other. Not everyone in this world is going to like you, and that's okay. We don't have to please everyone—it's most important to be happy with ourselves. So even if someone doesn't like you, it doesn't mean that you're not a good person or that you're not good enough. Remind yourself that there are people you don't like either, and there's nothing wrong with that. You just aren't compatible, and probably not meant to like each other because of how different you are. We're all unique, and we need to accept that not everyone is going to like our uniqueness.

Our thoughts tend to go negative when we make mistakes. We talk ourselves down and make ourselves feel bad just because of a single thing we did. This can only lead to making us feel worse about ourselves, and it won't help us to be positive, either. Therefore, we must shut out our negative thoughts and welcome positive ones in. Instead of saying, "I didn't study enough so now I'm going to fail the test," say, "I tried my best and will do the best I can today on the test."

Negativity isn't going to get you anywhere, and it'll only make you feel worse about yourself. Instead of thinking negatively about a situation, try looking at the facts of what happened. It's often not as bad as you make it sound or as your thoughts turn it into. When you look objectively at what happened, it might make you realize that it's okay and it'll get better.

Give yourself time to take breaks and have fun. We're too hard on ourselves, and only allow ourselves productivity and hard work. We're not robots. We need time off of work to be productive again. Give yourself time to take a break and reset. Loving yourself is all about knowing what you need from yourself and what you can do to recharge and be ready for the day. There's nothing wrong with treating yourself once in a while.

We don't love ourselves because we feel that we should have the life someone else has. We compare ourselves to others because we feel like we should be as successful as they are at this stage of our lives, but this is wrong. Every person has their own timeline and shouldn't follow the same route as everyone else. Just because your friend got a degree at 22 doesn't mean you have to. Just because they got married and have a child on the way doesn't mean you have to. Their life is different from yours, and that's the way it should be. Everyone will reach their dreams and become successful in their own time. Make sure to remind yourself of that.

Allow yourself to set boundaries and say no when you feel you need to. When you set clear rules for yourself, it gives you power over your life. If you're steadfast in your choices, it makes you feel more confident. Also, when someone breaks your set rules or when you don't like something they do, don't be afraid to stand up for yourself. When you do, you'll feel proud of yourself and gain more confidence to be yourself.

When you feel that you're constantly talking negatively about yourself and you can't get out of that space, you can reach out to others for help. Surround yourself with positive people who will listen to you and help you through the tough times. Often when we struggle, we shut ourselves off from the world because we don't want to ask for help, but this is exactly the opposite of what we should do. People who you trust and who are good for you are always there to help and make you feel better. By asking for help, you're already on the right track to loving yourself.

Remember that self-love is a journey. It isn't a simple task that can easily be ticked off a list—it's a process that has a lot of ups and downs, but it's worthwhile to go through. And when you finally reach a place where you're happy with yourself, celebrate this victory. It's a huge accomplishment, and you should be proud of it!

These are just some important things you can do to love yourself more and work on being your confident and happy self. In this chapter, we've highlighted the following:

- Who "The One" is
- Whether we have to find "The One"
- How we attract "The One"
- How you are "The One"
- How you can love yourself before loving others

When you love yourself, it gives you the confidence to find a partner. Finding "The One" isn't necessarily the end goal, but you can find a partner that suits you well even without being perfect.

Now that we've looked at who "The One" is and what you can do to love them, we'll discuss how you can connect with others. In chapter six, you'll learn the techniques you need to succeed in love and connect with the people you truly care about.

# Part 2

*Techniques to Succeed in Love*

# Chapter 6: How to Connect with Anyone

♡

---

Love, in its essence, is spiritual fire.
- **Seneca**

Forming a connection is an important part of any relationship, romantic or not. When you connect with each other, it creates a strong bond between you and can help kick off the romantic relationship. A way to understand how to connect with someone else is by understanding their love languages. Not only will we look at what these love languages are, but we'll also look at how you can notice them and what to do once you understand them.

Creating a deep connection has a lot to do with communication; when you communicate, you can discover the things that will create a strong connection between you and your partner. Therefore, we'll go into how to communicate and how this will help you create that connection. Lastly, I'll give some tips on how to connect and how this can benefit any relationship.

## The Love Languages

The five love languages are a way to connect to and understand your partner. A love language is what makes your partner happy and is the way that they give and receive love. Each person has a certain love language they use to express their love, and it's different for everyone. When you discover your partner's love language, it can help you form a strong connection with them. Let's look at the five different types to help us understand how each person connects with others.

## Words Of Affirmation

Have you ever wondered why some people blush when you say something nice to them, and others simply shrug it off? These two people have different love languages. For those who like words of affirmation, compliments and kind words are very important to them. When they receive these things, it boosts their mood significantly. They get shy when they receive compliments because they mean a lot to them, and when they're struggling, a kind word can lighten up their day. When they receive a kind comment, they may remember it for a long time.

Simple words that show acknowledgement and kindness are very effective. Therefore, when communicating with someone who likes words of affirmation, you can bond with them by giving them genuine, heartfelt compliments and kind words.

However, they also don't take harsh words lightly. Be careful what you say to them, as negative words can affect them for a long time.

## Physical Touch

Physical touch doesn't necessarily mean sensual physical touch. It's the small things that matter the most. For those who subscribe to this love language, physical touch is very important. It can be as simple as a hand on the shoulder or a touch on the back. For these people, they'll develop a strong connection with someone if they receive or give physical touch. Physical touch is a way for them to acknowledge others, and when they receive it back they feel loved and acknowledged.

It means a lot to them when you hold their hand, give them hugs, and kiss them. When they don't receive any physical touch, they'll feel uncertain. Receiving it from their partner often will make them feel confident, happy, and loved.

## Acts of Service

For these types of people, they feel loved and recognised when people help them with things or do things for them. This could be anything from opening the car door to washing the dishes. An extra hand always makes them smile and feel appreciated.

Whenever they have to do something that isn't always fun, helping them out makes the task easier, and they'll feel more positive and happy because of it. When they do nice things for others, this is their way of showing they care and want to connect with you. By doing things for others, they're also helping themselves.

## Quality Time

These types of people feel loved when they have quality alone time with others. When they talk to others or when others make time to talk to them, they feel joy. They like to listen and acknowledge others by listening. They form a bond with others by talking and discovering more about them as a person.

For them, undivided attention is important. It shows them that you care and want to listen to them. You shouldn't let anything distract you when you talk to someone whose love language is quality time. Try not to be on your phone or busy with something else while they want to talk to you. It makes them feel unheard and may make them feel that you don't want to spend time with them.

To connect with them, spend a good amount of time talking, listening, and doing fun things together while getting to know them better.

## Gift Giving

For some, gift giving is important. They like to put thought into the gifts they give to others, and they also want thoughtful and meaningful gifts in return. A gift is a way to show someone you care. If you give a gift, it can show that you care.

If they receive a silly or thoughtless gift, they might feel you don't know or understand them. Or, if you don't give any gift at all when they expect one, they'll feel forgotten and unimportant. They also enjoy giving thoughtful gifts to others. When they see that you're happy with the gift they gave, they feel loved and happy.

Giving the right gift to a person whose love language is gift giving is important. It shows them that you listen to what they say and that you know them well. Put thought into what you're giving them and make an effort to buy a personalized gift for them.

## How To Notice Love Languages

The best way to notice someone's love languages is to look out for them. Think about previous instances where one of these five love languages was present. Think of what your partner has been receptive to: Do they like it when you give compliments? Were they over the moon with a gift you gave them? Do they like to touch your arm often or hold your hand as much as possible? Are they annoyed and tell you to put your phone away when you talk to them? Is it important to them that you're placing your focus solely on them when they talk? Do they like helping you when you don't even ask them to?

Be observant in noticing certain habits they have. Finding their love language will take some time to figure out, but when you do, try to communicate to them through it.

You can also take time to think about what your own love languages are. Think of what you relate to most after reading the five descriptions. When you understand your partner's love languages, practice them. This helps to create a strong connection. If you're struggling to notice a love language in your partner, it's never wrong to ask them what they like most. Communication always helps to understand your partner's needs.

## Communication Tips

The best way to connect with anyone is through communication. Communicating will help you understand and learn more about them. This applies to anyone you want to build a relationship with, no matter what sort of relationship you want with them. Let's look at a few ways you can improve your communication skills and effectively talk and engage with people.

When communicating, understand what the other person is saying before you respond. Sometimes we jump into a conversation without even knowing the context, or we speak before someone else has finished speaking. They haven't even explained themselves, and yet sometimes we assume we already know what they're going to say. When you're having a conversation, don't rush it. Take your time to hear what the other person is saying and respond after you've thought their words through. Listen to them and form your sentences in your brain but try not to interrupt them. This is difficult to do because sometimes, if you don't interrupt them, you can't get a word out. However, make sure they feel like they've said enough before you talk.

Communicating well isn't only about talking, it's about showing that you listen. What I mean by this is that your body language is just as important as your words. When you turn away from them while talking or don't make eye contact, it can make them feel that you aren't listening or don't want to listen.

When communicating, make eye contact every now and then and face the person you're communicating with. Also, opening your arms instead of crossing them in front of you makes others feel more welcome, and makes you seem happy to talk to them. People immediately pick up on when others don't want to talk to them or aren't interested, and that's because of body language.

When you listen, you must try to understand what emotions people are going through. When people are vulnerable and open up to you, try to imagine the way they feel. Even if you think they're upset about something silly, don't be insensitive and tell them it's silly. Make them feel heard and try to understand their situation. It's hard to understand how others are feeling, but if you show them, you're at least trying and that you're being respectful, they'll appreciate it. They'll want to communicate with you more if they feel understood.

When you're upset with someone about something they did to annoy you, be sure to talk to them about it.

However, you should also find the right time to do it. It won't end well if you try to communicate with someone about something that went wrong when they've had a horrible day and aren't feeling the best. Instead of bombarding them with more things that may upset them, choose the right time to talk about the issue. This could be when you spend quality time together or when there's time to relax and not think about anything else. Talk calmly about the problem and explain it thoroughly. You don't want it to turn into an argument. Be calm and think about what you want to say clearly.

Using the right words is also very important. When you talk without thinking, you might end up saying something you didn't mean to, and your words can easily be taken the wrong way. Think of the right words at the right time before you speak. This can help avoid arguments and misunderstandings.

Don't be afraid to ask questions when you feel the need to. Responding with simple words like 'yes' and 'okay' lets someone know that you're actively listening. When you ask questions, it helps them realize you want to understand what they're saying. You might also find yourself more interested and engaged in the conversation when you ask questions and use simple words to reply. It not only helps you to listen properly, but it also makes them want to communicate with you, too.

There's nothing wrong with a bit of silence when talking. Use that silence to formulate your sentences and words before you continue speaking. Don't let silence intimidate you.

Communicate more than you think you should.

Sometimes a sentence makes sense in your head, but it doesn't make any sense to others when you say it aloud. This is just because our brains work differently. It doesn't mean you can't form comprehending sentences, it just means that everyone understands things differently. So when someone's confused, make sure you can explain what you're saying in a different way. Something else might make more sense to them than your original sentence. Try to describe your thoughts in different words and communicate in a way they understand.

When you're struggling to explain your feelings or to communicate well with your partner, start your sentence with 'I.' We're quick to blame others instead of explaining what we feel and why we feel it. When we start our sentences with 'I,' we explain our feelings without blaming anyone else. This helps you to communicate well and avoid arguments.

These communication skills will not only help you communicate with others well, they'll also specifically help you communicate with your partner. And without communication skills, it won't be easy to form a connection. Let's figure out how we can form a connection with the new skills we've learned, and how this connection can help us create a strong bond with anyone.

## Connection Tips

When you connect with others, you become closer to them. A connection allows you to respect each other, understand each other, and care for each other. Connecting with others is understanding them on a deeper level. It's supporting them, showing them, you understand, and respecting them as a person. When you connect with someone, you can be open and vulnerable, and they feel the same toward you. You trust them, and they make you feel appreciated. So how can we connect with others and make them feel understood?

When you want to connect with others, they must feel that you want to connect with them. The best way to invite people to have a conversation is to smile. Smiling makes others feel comforted and like they're welcome. It invites them to learn more about you. When you smile at someone, it generally evokes positive emotions, and it's a good start to forming a bond.

To form a connection, you have to get to know people. That means you have to spend quality time with them to learn more about them. The more you know about them, the more you can relate to them. Once you find things you have in common, it's easier to form a stronger bond.

If you've already known this person for a while, don't be afraid to find out more about them. Ask them about deeper things, and about things that mean a lot to them in their life. If you want to connect with them, ask them about things they enjoy. It will show that you care and that you want to learn more about their likes and dislikes. Even if you think you know them, search deeper to find out even more. People appreciate it when others are interested in them.

The only way you can create a genuine connection is by being truthful and honest. If you're being something you're not in front of them, they'll notice that, and there will be a wall put up between you. If you want a connection and a bond, be okay with being yourself.

Another way you can connect is by reaching out to them. If you haven't seen them in a while, reach out to them and let them know you're available to talk. When you make yourself available, it shows them that you want to continue to form a connection and that you care. You can reach out to them by phone call or by setting up a visit. Even when you see them coincidentally, greet them and talk to them. If you want to connect with someone, stay connected.

If they reach out to you or do things for you, show them that you appreciate them. Showing your appreciation will make them feel like they want to connect with you and keep you in their life. For example, if they bring you chocolates, thank them and tell them how grateful you are.

To connect with others, don't just try to impress them. It doesn't help to pretend that you know everything in the world. People don't like it when you try to impress them with things you know nothing about. They'll quickly realize how clueless you are. Talk about things you know and understand. When they bring something up that you don't understand, don't pretend like you know everything about it. Be honest—they'll appreciate this honesty.

Physical touch also helps. It doesn't have to be romantic; a hug or a pat on the shoulder shows you care. Some form of physical connection shows them that your focus is on them and that you're there for them. Any physical touch generally makes people feel noticed and loved unless they dislike this type of love language. Make sure that they're the type of person who appreciates this before you squeeze them tightly. It's important to show respect, too.

Show them support and congratulate them on their achievements. Make sure not to be jealous about their accomplishments or make them feel insignificant because of them. When something good happens to them, show your support. This will make them feel good about their accomplishments and proud of themselves. They're also more likely to share these accomplishments with you when you're happy for them.

In this chapter, we've highlighted the following:

- The five different types of love languages
- How to notice your and others' love languages
- How to communicate well
- How to connect with others

Now that you understand these topics, we can get into the details of a romantic relationship. It was important to first realize how you should communicate with anyone you want to connect with, and how to form that connection with them in the first place.

In chapter seven, we'll look into dating and the survival guide you need on how to navigate romantic love. We'll start off with the first date and everything you need to know about it. We'll then move on to when the right time is for a first kiss, and, finally, making it official. Let's jump right into the exciting world of a new relationship.

# Chapter 7: Dating Survival Guide

♡

---

We can only learn to love by loving.
**- Iris Murdoch**

This is your dating survival guide that will help make relationships and dating that much less intimidating. It can be scary and difficult, but once we get past the fear of first dates and the uncertainty of beginning a new relationship, we can reap the benefits of love.

Now that we've looked at how to form a strong connection, we need to understand how to turn that into something romantic. This can be daunting because you don't know what the other person is thinking or feeling. This uncertainty makes rejection possible, and it makes it more difficult to commit and put your heart on the line. With this dating guide, it'll feel slightly easier to jump into the world of dating.

Let's start where first impressions matter: The world of first dates.

## The First Date

The first date is an important part of dating. Unfortunately, we can't get away from them. It's inevitable to have a first date, and you must have one if you want to start dating. The first date is daunting, but just remember, if they dislike you for who you are, then they're not the one for you.

Before you go on a first date, there are a few things that need to happen beforehand. You must be interested in each other, and you must actually ask or be asked out on the date. There must be interest before anything else can happen. So how do you know whether they want to go on a first date with you?

## Are They Interested?

Maybe you think the person who keeps looking over at you is interested, but you're unsure, and therefore you let it go. But what if it could have been something great? How do you know if someone is interested in you? And if they aren't, or you're unsure, how do you gauge their interest?

There are many different ways to notice whether someone is interested in you or not. The first and most obvious is eye contact; there's a difference between friendly eye contact in conversation and eye contact that shows someone likes you. When someone likes you, they're oftentimes quite shy about it, so you might catch them looking at you more than once. Maybe every time you look, you see them already looking. They immediately look away, however, and try not to look suspicious.

If someone isn't interested, they'll only look once and

move on. However, you'll catch a person who's interested in you looking at you more than what's normal. Some eyes might flit away quickly, while others might try to hold your gaze longer. It depends on how brave that person is.

Often, when someone is interested, they want to be as close to you as possible without making you feel uncomfortable. They might lean closer to you when they talk, turn their body toward you, stand next to you everywhere you go, or touch you whenever they can. An accidental slide of the hand against yours, a soft punch to your shoulder when you make a joke, a hug, a hand on the back; anything physical that's still respectful.

When they like you, they're very interested in you and your life. They ask you lots of questions because shared interests excite them, and your stories fascinate them. Even if your interests aren't very similar, they'll make an effort to relate to them. For example, even though they prefer video games, they'll tell you how amazing board games are and their favorite ones if you bring them up. They'll laugh at anything you say (even when you're not that funny). They also ask your opinion on certain things in their life, and they value your words and judgment.

They smile, and their eyes light up when they see you. Their smile lasts longer than a regular smile, and they're genuinely happy to see you. They give you compliments and take notice of small things; for example, the new earrings you're wearing or the haircut you got.

They want to spend loads of time with you, even when you're not around. They might stay up late talking over the phone with you or text you late at night even when they know they have to wake up early. They just want to know what's going on in your life and they want to be involved.

If you want someone to be interested in you, you must show that you're interested, too. Be yourself and be honest, but don't try too hard. If you do, you become something you're not. You can use these techniques to show that you're interested in them, too. If they don't respond after you've tried your best, let it go. Not everyone will be interested in you, and that's okay.

**The Invitation**

Once you've established that they're interested or you've shown that you're interested, the invitation to the first date is the next step. How do you ask someone out on a first date? How do you take that leap of faith and hope that the answer is yes?

When you want to ask someone out on a date, it's good to talk to them first to form a connection. Try not to use small talk and ask interesting, friendly questions rather than what they think of the weather today. Make jokes and be lighthearted. Try to keep it playful and flirty, although being flirty with someone you like can be quite hard. Once you've spoken for a while and you're relaxed, just go for it.

Don't overthink it and be straightforward. Be specific when asking the question so that they know you're going to follow through. Tell them what day and what activity you're proposing to do. For example, "Do you want to go out for coffee with me sometime this weekend? Let's say Saturday?" If they respond negatively to this and reject your invitation, don't take it to heart. It's probably for the best that you find out how they feel earlier rather than later. You have to be able to move on.

I prefer talking to a person in real life instead of on the phone, but if you are, read their reply carefully. If they seem excited then you're good to go, but if they seem vague and give short replies, they might only be accepting out of kindness. Even if they do, I advise to still go on the date and decide afterwards whether there's interest there or not.

## First Date Ideas

I believe that a first date should be something fun that both parties can enjoy and where you can build a connection. Sure, a movie is great, but the idea of a first date is to actually get to know each other and to decide whether or not you like this person so much that you want to go on a second date with them.

My advice would be to find something that both of you are interested in. If you go for a classic date at a restaurant, choose somewhere that serves your date's favorite food. If you both like being active, a walk on the beach or at the park is a great way to bond, although it depends on how well you know each other. If you don't know each other very well yet, stick to going somewhere public. Go bowling or ice-skating and catch a meal afterwards. Do something that's memorable, but not too over-the-top; something casual and fun. When we overthink it and head out to a fancy restaurant, it might make our date feel that our expectations are high, and that a casual date wouldn't be good enough.

Other first date ideas include:

- going to a theme park/waterpark
- going to a concert
- going mini-golfing
- going to an arcade
- going to an event

These ideas are perfect if you're looking for something adventurous, but there's nothing wrong with a simple dinner date.

## Questions to Deepen the Connection

It's important to ask questions to show that you're interested and want to find out more about this person. However, your first date shouldn't feel like an interview. It should be casual and fun, and questions should come up naturally. Don't ask questions that are too hard. Some may ask questions that their dates don't know how to answer, and it puts them in an awkward position. Make sure your questions aren't difficult nor only require a 'yes' or 'no' answer.

Make sure that you can start a conversation with the questions you're asking. The date shouldn't be filled with questions. A really fantastic question would be one that kick-starts a long conversation. After hours, the date is already done, and it will have felt quick because you've been talking for hours. This can happen all because of one good question!

Of course, this doesn't always happen, but spacing out questions can help it feel more casual and not too much like an interview. The questions you ask should be a mixture of deep and meaningful with silly and playful. If the first date is too deep, it can make the other person feel uncomfortable, and if it's too playful, it can leave you wondering if your date doesn't enjoy talking about deep topics. There's a lot to think about, but make sure not to think too much. Every first date is different. If the words flow naturally without any questions at all, let it flow. You must figure out what the mood is and when the appropriate time is to ask questions. It's not as hard as it sounds. Just think of it as a normal conversation because it is. You're getting to know each other as you normally would with anyone else.

Also let them ask you questions and be open to answering them. This will keep it from turning into an interview. Here are some questions and topics you can discuss on the first date:

- Ask about likes and dislikes. See if you have any similarities you can talk about.
- Ask them about their favorite place they've ever gone to.
- Ask about something they've done that they're proud of.
- Ask them about their family and who they're closest to.
- Ask them about one interesting thing that most people don't know about them.
- Ask them silly questions that will make them laugh. For example, "Would you rather be locked

up in a cage with a million bugs, or have 10 bees swarming around you?"

There are many topics you can jump into. You can talk about deeper things, such as certain beliefs and values, but make sure to balance it out with fun and silly ones, too.

## Reframing Rejection

If, after you've gone on the first date and they've decided that they don't want to have a second date, don't be discouraged. This also goes for if they've rejected the first date. I know everyone is terrified of rejection and therefore scared of dating, but it doesn't have to be such a scary thing.

Rejection is a part of life. You get rejected for jobs and by different people. You'll experience rejection more than once in life, and you have to learn to be okay with that. Rejection is good because it shows us that something isn't what we were meant to be doing. For example, if you don't get the job, don't be discouraged. That position just wasn't for you, and now you might get a job that's much better than what you imagined. When someone rejects you, that person just wasn't meant for you at that time of your life. You'll find someone else who's good for you and will treat you much better than they ever could.

We have to take rejection as a learning experience. Every relationship was meant to happen because we learn from them, but not every relationship was meant to last. If you get rejected for a second date, it's a good thing. You don't want to waste your time on someone who doesn't feel the same about you.

I'm not saying that it's easy to move on, I'm just saying that we need to try to take the rejection with a pinch of salt. Don't let it ruin your life. Relax, and tell yourself to stay calm. Not all hope is lost. You'll get through it and will come out the other side a better person.

# The First Kiss

The first kiss can be scary. What if your partner doesn't like it? What if they don't want to be kissed? When's the right time for the kiss? Are you even a good kisser? All these thoughts might be floating around in your head when you're in love and want to take the relationship to the next level. It's good if you have these questions, because it means that you're ready to take the next step and you want something to happen. But how do you know if they want something to happen, too?

## The Right Moment

The right moment for a kiss is difficult to pinpoint. Every situation is different. But it also depends on how the actual date is going. If you're both enjoying your time and there are some long, electric moments between the two of you, it might be the right time for a kiss. But when you feel that the date isn't going great and that you want to leave as soon as possible, you should probably avoid kissing.

You can detect the right moment for a kiss by looking at the person's body language and behavior. If they get close to you, keep looking at you, and want to keep eye contact, they might be hinting that they want to be kissed.

Try to detect the atmosphere of the date. Is it lighthearted, playful, and flirty, or is it uncomfortable, silent, and difficult? If it's the latter, you'll most likely not want to kiss. Just remember that you're both nervous for this kiss, and it's normal to be this nervous. It shows how much you each like each other and that you both want it to go well. Unfortunately, kissing isn't a sport, so I can't really coach you on when the right time is for one.

However, you can control where the kiss should happen. A kiss is an intimate thing. Kissing them shouldn't feel awkward because others are watching. Find a time where you feel comfortable to kiss. Find a moment that feels romantic. It could be while you're sitting on the couch talking, when you say goodbye, or at the dinner table surrounded by candlelight. You have to decide based on the feel of the atmosphere.

A way to figure out whether to make the move or not is to move closer. If they feel uncomfortable and move away, that means they're probably not ready for the kiss. It doesn't necessarily mean that they don't like you but might just mean that they feel like it isn't the right moment. Instead of building it up in your head as a nerve-wracking experience, turn it into something exciting that you look forward to.

The more you kiss, the easier it gets, so don't put too much pressure on the first kiss. We all want a magical moment, but maybe the magical moment will happen on the second or third kiss instead. Rather than building it up too much in your head, let the moment happen, and don't be disappointed when it's awkward at first. With the right person, kisses will feel magical, even if the first one wasn't so great.

**Making It Memorable**

Once the kiss happens, how do we make it memorable? For a kiss to be effective, you must live in the moment. Keep your mind fixed solely on your partner. It makes the kiss more memorable to you, and probably for your partner, too.

Everyone likes different types of kisses, and you won't know until you try. However, don't jump into things too fast. For the first kiss, make sure it's tender and passionate. Try holding the kiss for a moment longer than what would be normal. This makes the kiss linger when it's gone and makes it that much more magical. Also, before going for the kiss on the mouth, a kiss on the neck or cheek can be a great lead up to it. It will leave your partner wanting more, and they'll be ready for one on the lips.

To make sure the kiss is great, make sure your breath smells good and your lips are soft. Kissing is all about the feel of the kiss; if their lips are dry, you likely wouldn't want to kiss them again.

A kiss is more memorable when you do more than just kiss: What I mean by this is using your hands to add to the kiss. I know my heart just bursts open when my partner holds me by the neck when we're kissing or caresses my back. Using your hands as an extra physical touch can make the first kiss unforgettable.

Try these things to leave a lasting impression on your love interest. Who knows, they might even want to make it official after an electrifying kiss!

## Making It Official

Once you've moved past the scary first date and maybe even the first kiss, it's time to make it official. A first date should happen before making it official, but a first kiss can happen either before or after. However, the sequence of events go, if you really like this person, it's time to think about taking it a step further. If you want to keep spending time with them and you can't stop thinking about them, it's probably time to take your relationship to the next level. So how do we take it to the next level, and how do we know the right time for it?

### Labeling the Relationship

If you feel you long for this person and can't keep your eyes off of them, it's probably time to make it official. For that to happen, you must know where you both stand and what you both want. This doesn't mean you have to have everything figured out, but it's good to know what your love interest thinks about relationships.

The best way to ask someone to become official is to be as open and honest as possible. Say what you mean, and make sure they understand what you're saying. Simply say that you'd like to see where this takes you, and that you want to take the relationship one step further. Tell them you want to make it official and ask them how they feel about it. Showing your vulnerability shows that you care and that you're willing to open up for them.

Have a conversation about what your values and boundaries are and speak honestly about what you expect out of the relationship. Honesty is a great building block for the start of a new relationship.

## Aligning on Expectations

Before jumping into a relationship, it's good to figure out if your expectations align. What do you want out of the relationship? Do you see a future for the relationship? These are hard questions that you have to ask yourself as well as the other person in order to understand where you both stand when it comes to relationships.

The way for a relationship to work is to talk about the expectations you have and to see how you can align your expectations with one another. If you feel like they're expecting too much from you at the start, be honest and talk about how you can work through it to align your expectations rather than work against each other. Identify each other's expectations and talk about whether you agree or not.

If you can't come to an agreement, you can either work it out or decide not to engage in a relationship. For example, if they expect something that's against the boundaries you've set, then your values don't align, and it will be difficult to move past this.

The best thing you can do is to be as clear as possible. Aligning your expectations with each other will help you understand where you stand in the relationship, and this will help the relationship grow.

You can also talk about expectations once you've already started the relationship. This will help you see where they are in their life and how it can align with yours. For a relationship to work, you must work in tandem to build a life together. You must be able to have your own independent lives, but also create one together.

In this chapter, we've highlighted the following:

- how to know if someone is interested
- how to set up a first date
- how to look at rejection
- when the right moment is for a first kiss
- how to make the first kiss memorable
- how to make the relationship official

From first dates to first kisses, and to eventually starting a relationship, this is a daunting yet very exciting process. It's something we all have to go through if we want to have a relationship with someone. But instead of dreading it, you can learn to see the excitement and fun in it. Think of the great things that could happen if you take that leap. Be positive and believe that the right person will come your way even after you have failed attempts.

But what if all of this fails? Instead of a first date, what if you get placed in the friend zone? This is a scary thing that many people don't know what to do about. In chapter eight, I'll help you navigate this dangerous zone and come out happier on the other side.

*Chapter 8: The Friend Zone*

♡

This was the best date I'd ever been on. And it wasn't even a date.
- **Abby Jimenez**

# The dreaded friend zone.

We all worry that our crush only likes us as a friend and that we'll end up in a situation of unrequited love. We may have fallen in love with one of our friends, and don't know how to get out of the friend zone. Getting out of the friend zone is a tricky feat. It's a dangerous line to walk, but I'm here to help you trapeze over it brilliantly. Let's look at how friends can become more than friends, and how we can get out of the friend zone. Don't panic if you've developed feelings for your friend—there is a way to deal with it.

## What To Do When Falling In Love With A Friend

A friend is someone you spend loads of time with. You get to know every side of them, laugh with them, and share special moments with them often. Because you spend so much time together and you're so close, it's easy to fall in love with them. Maybe one day you stare at your best friend and realize that they're much better looking than you thought they were before. Feelings start to creep in, and you become more nervous around them. But what are you supposed to do about it? Are you really falling in love, or do you just think you're falling in love because you want to spend lots of time with them?

Firstly, stop and process your thoughts. Think clearly about your friend. Ask yourself, why are you falling in love with them? Think about how you see them differently now, what has changed, and if the feelings are true. Sometimes we experience waves of love for our friends, but it's only because we're so close with them and have strong positive feelings for our friends without it being romantic.

Think about whether these feelings you're experiencing are friendly fondness or romantic. Fond admiration is a feeling you experience within friendships, whereas romantic attraction is more than just friendship. Are you picturing kissing them and holding them? Do you like the way their body looks? Are you starting to think of them more sexually?

Once you've clearly gone through these emotions in your

head, look at your reactions towards your friend. Do you experience butterflies every time you see them? Do you become shy around them? Has your normal friendship dynamic changed? Monitor your reactions closely.

Once you've figured out whether you are really experiencing romantic feelings for this person, take your time. Don't rush into blurting out that you're in love with them. Think before you take any steps.

Next, you must see how your friend reacts. Look closely at how they're acting around you. It's difficult to realize whether they just want to stay friends or are hiding their feelings and want to be more. So, what you can do is to leave subtle hints and see how they react to them. How do they react when you move closer to them? How do they react when you make lots of eye contact? If they still react as a normal friend would, then unfortunately you're still in the dark about their feelings. When you develop these feelings, make sure not to be rude to your friend. It's not their fault that you're developing these feelings for them.

This is when you must make a decision: Do you risk it all by telling them, or do you ignore your feelings and continue to be friends with them? Let's look at the pros and cons of each scenario. When you tell them you have feelings for them, the following things can happen:

-They can reciprocate the feelings and it can turn into a romantic relationship.

-They can tell you they don't feel the same and the friendship dynamic can change.

-They can tell you they don't feel the same, but the friendship stays the same.

-They can think that you're joking, and this will

confirm that they only want to be friends.

An advantage of this is that at least you know where you stand in the relationship you have with them. However, the disadvantage is that it can change the strong friendship that you've built. The friendship dynamic might change into something awkward, and it might never be the same.

If you don't tell them, you have feelings for them, the following can happen:

- Your feelings can fade away and the friendship will remain the same.
- Your feelings will grow stronger, making it more difficult to hide these feelings and to live with them.

The advantage to this is that your friendship will remain strong. The disadvantage is that your feelings can eat you alive, making you sad and depressed.

Now comes the part where you'll have to make a decision. Will you risk your friendship and tell them your feelings, or will you ignore the feelings and hope they go away? This is a decision that only you can make. Assess the situation and make the decision based on it.

Once you've made the decision, be confident with it. Stick to

this decision, and no matter what the outcome is, be proud of the choice you've made. If you realize that the decision isn't working, you can always change it, but be confident and try it out first before changing your mind.

The last part is to act. Once you've made your decision, you must follow through with your actions. If you don't want to tell them, find ways to get over your feelings, such as spending more time with other friends and doing activities with them that aren't related to romance at all, or spend more time doing things you love to do on your own. Write your thoughts down in a journal as a way to release them without telling them to your friend.

If it means seeing your friend a little bit less than normal to get over these feelings, then do so. However, it doesn't mean you have to change the dynamic in your friendship. If you can stay friends while trying to let these feelings go, that's great. But if you can't, that's okay too.

If you decide that you can't keep your feelings in, it's better to tell them. But how should you go about doing this?

## How To Tell Them

There's no easy way to tell your friend that you have feelings for them. It might end up going exactly the way you wanted, or it might go the opposite. However, if you never say anything, you might feel worse about it than you do now. You're going to have to decide when the time is right to do it. I would suggest you tell them when you're alone, so that no one else can get in the way when you're talking. Find a place where you're both relaxed and where the atmosphere is stress free.

Don't tell them beforehand that there's something important you have to say. This will just make them stress and freak out about it before you've even started the conversation. Start with a casual and lighthearted talk. Doing things that are out of the ordinary will just make them uneasy.

Try to stop yourself from overthinking. The more you think about it, the more what-if scenarios you'll conjure up in your head, and the more scared you'll get. Think about it in a straightforward way: You'll hang out with your friend and talk about your feelings. It'll be a normal conversation, and no matter what the outcome is, you'll survive it.

I would suggest also telling them as soon as you can. After making the decision that you're going to tell them, don't stretch out the time between telling them and waiting for the right moment. The longer you wait, the harder it's going to be to let them know. Just get it out of the way as soon as you can. Sometimes, the right moment is now.

It often helps to work up the courage before speaking to your friend. List your positive qualities, and ask others what your positive qualities are. This will help you see that you can be confident and have the courage and strength to get through this. If someone can help you hype yourself up, it can help you to talk about your feelings.

Make sure that, when you're talking, you get to the point quickly.

Let them know what the conversation is about, but also let them know that there's no pressure to talk back. You just want to tell them about your feelings, and they don't have to respond right away. Put the pressure off of them and simply tell them what you're feeling. Don't go and write a script for what you're planning to say. If you talk like it's a presentation, it might not come through as genuine, and they'll see it as a joke rather than something serious.

If you've been putting it off for too long, make a due date

for yourself. Tell yourself that you must tell them by a certain day. This will put pressure on you to get it done and over with. After you've told them you liked them, don't expect anything from them. Give them some space, and give yourself a break from thinking about it.

When telling them your feelings, keep it short and simple. Don't go into too much detail yet. They don't want to know when the feelings started or for how long this has been going on; they just have to process the information first. Unless they ask you questions, don't tell them more than you have to.

Always be optimistic about the situation, but at the same time, don't get your hopes up too high. Congratulate yourself for telling them and getting it out of the way. Be proud of yourself for handling it well, and tell yourself no matter the outcome, you were very brave.

Getting support from others is also a good way to help you tell your friend you have feelings for them. Another friend can encourage and motivate you, and they can help you muster up the courage. Your friend can help you figure out whether they like you back or not. They can give subtle hints to your friend to figure out if this friend likes you back. Make sure that you reveal your feelings to someone you trust. They can help you get through it and give you encouragement to take the final step.

No matter how awful you feel after telling this person, it will get better, and it's usually not as bad as it seems. If they don't like you in that way, it's probably for the best, and at least you got your feelings off of your chest.

There are times where you end up in the friend zone accidentally. Maybe you've noticed this friend likes you, but they think you don't like them back. So how do you get out of this tricky area called the friend zone?

# How To Get Out Of The Friend Zone

Let's say that you have a crush on someone, and you think they like you, too. However, they're very oblivious to the fact that you like them and are keeping you in the friend zone because they think you want them to. Maybe you're stuck in the friend zone because you don't know what the next step is and how to move it further along. Let's look at ways we can escape the friend zone and turn a crush into a relationship, or just to let them know what you're feeling. It's a difficult situation to be in, but we can climb out of this hole we're in and become happier because of it.

To escape the friend zone, you have to gain confidence in yourself and become someone they'd love to be around. To do this, make sure to always look and smell good. I'm not saying you should be something you're not, but rather to be the best version of yourself. With friends, we often don't really care how we look, and we reveal our bad habits to them. This places you deep in the friend zone. It prevents them from thinking about you romantically. Therefore, put an effort into making yourself look good. They'll definitely notice this change. If they ask why, you look different, tell them that you're doing it for yourself, which is partly true. Self-confidence is very sexy.

Try out a new wardrobe that you feel comfortable in but also look good in. Enhance the good qualities you have and make them look twice when you walk past. But don't overdo it. It might come off as weird and over-the-top, and they might not know how to react.

Be the person they would want to date. If they're looking for someone kind and caring, show these traits off. Don't be someone you're not but enhance the good qualities that you have. It can show them that you can be not only a good friend, but a loving person, too.

Give them genuine compliments, encouragement, and support. This can make them feel loved, and they'll want more of this love. Being happy and kind puts them in a good mood, too, and it makes them think about why they feel so happy around you.

A way you can also make yourself more desirable is by distancing yourself from them. Instead of always being available, let them know that you aren't always free and that you have other things going on in your life. Making yourself seem less desperate makes them want to see you more. It makes them want to work to see you.

A way to get yourself out of the friend zone is to do less. Show that you're less interested in them—it's twisted reverse therapy, but it often makes them want to see you more, wonder what they did wrong, and think about what more they can do to get your attention.

Go do fun activities with them. An adrenaline boost will often make them feel happier around you, and this will make them want to see you more. You can also touch them more; a pat on the arm or a playful punch can help them bond with you, and this can help to grow the interest even stronger. Make sure you make lots of eye contact with them. Staring deep into their eyes will help them notice that you want to become more than friends. And it will make them think about it, too.

Ask them to do things for you. Don't be too pushy but ask them for help here and there. If they're into you, they'll want to do favors for you and help you out with tasks.

One of the best ways to get out of the friend zone is to make them feel jealous. Spend time with other people, and make sure they know about this. Don't be cruel but show them that you have other people in your life, too. Start dating or tell them you're open to dating. If they don't want you in the friend zone anymore, they'll be intimidated about these dates and will want to get your attention. You'll notice if they become jealous when they get uncomfortable when you talk about dates or get annoyed when you talk about the dates you went on.

Although, don't force your way out of the friend zone when you see that they really just want to stay friends. Be the friend that they want. Don't push it too much, and don't expect anything from them. Be okay with the outcome, regardless of how difficult it is.

Most importantly, focus on yourself and the goals you have. This can also get you out of the friend zone. Spend time on yourself. If they see you working on yourself, they might be more interested in your life and what's going on with it. Even if it doesn't work, at least you're focusing on what you want. Make sure your life is filled with other things, and you're not just hung up on the person who's friendzoning you.

These aren't definite, surefire ways to get out of the friend zone. However, if after you've done all these things you're still stuck in the friend zone, either they're blind or they're ignoring romance and focusing on your friendship. This is probably the best sign that you should stay friends. Remember that you can also just tell them about your feelings. Who knows, maybe this person is really just clueless, and they're madly in love with you!

In this chapter, we've highlighted the following:

- What to do when you're falling in love with a friend
- How to tell them
- How to break free from the friend zone
- What to do if you don't get out of the friend zone

When we can't get out of the friend zone, it's very hard to get over it. In fact, any type of rejection causes pain, such as breakups, loss, and any heartache in general. But to move on with life, we have to get over these rejections. If we fall in love with our friend and can't get out of the friend zone, or if we tell them about our feelings and they don't reciprocate, we're left in tatters. So how can we pick up the pieces and continue to be happy and thrive in life? In chapter nine, we'll look at the ways to get over heartbreak. The good news is there are ways to survive rejection, and there are things you can do to make it all feel better.

# Chapter 9: How to Get Over Rejection and Thrive

♡

---

Sometimes good things fall apart so better things can fall together.
**- Marilyn Monroe**

There's no denying that breakups are the worst. Getting rejected is tough for everyone, no matter how strong you are. All human beings want is to make connections with others, and when a connection gets rejected, we feel sad and depressed. We often feel like we're not good enough, and doubt clouds our minds when rejection comes our way.

Unfortunately, life is filled with rejections. There's not one person that has never been rejected for anything. Everyone has to experience this at least once in life. For some it might feel like the end of the world, while others take it in stride. So how can we all learn to take it in stride when we get rejected? How can we thrive and continue life as our happy and positive selves?

Before we discover how to move on with our lives, we have to discuss the pain heartbreak causes. You need to know that it's normal and that it hurts immensely, even when we don't want it to.

## Why Does It Hurt So Much?

When you open yourself up to people, there's always a risk of rejection. That's the risk of being vulnerable; either a lot of good can come out of it or you can get hurt in the process. Many things require risk: applying for college or a new job, asking someone out on a date, being in a relationship, and more. Anything that has to do with the heart and your emotions is a risk. But these are risks we have to take to find the happiness we want in life. If you never take risks, you stay stagnant in life, and it can become boring. We have to be able to take the pain.

Rejection and breakups hurt so much for multiple reasons. Emotional pain feels like physical pain, because the physical pain areas in our brains are triggered even when it's only emotional. Like we've learned in chapter one, just like the brain and body react to feelings of love, they also react to feelings of rejection. When our hearts ache, we physically experience the pain of loss and heartbreak. Because humans seek connection, we're unfortunately just wired this way. It's in our nature to want to be with others. When we're alone, we often experience feelings of loneliness, and it brings us physical pain, too. This is what makes humans so complex, because both emotional and physical sides work together.

Emotional pain also lasts longer than physical pain. When you experience heartache because of the loss of a loved one, it takes months or even years to fully recover from it. This also occurs in breakups. After spending all your time with someone and they decide to suddenly leave, it can be devastating. Many people say that time heals wounds, and it's true. The further you are from the experience, the less it affects you.

Think about a time where you got hurt. When I was younger, I fell off a bicycle and scraped my hand against the concrete. I still have the scar, but I can't remember how the pain of it felt. However, when I think of a breakup I had when I was younger, I still feel a bit of that emotional pain. I remember exactly how I felt when it happened. I remember how I struggled to eat and sleep, and how long it took me to get over it. This is just one example of how emotional pain lasts longer than physical pain. Think about any instance you had where something similar happened to you.

When we get rejected, we often beat ourselves up. Our thoughts can be really cruel. Even if it wasn't our fault, we blame ourselves for a breakup and think about what we did wrong. Our thoughts run wild, and we tell ourselves that we'll be single forever and that no one will love us. We think that no one likes us and that no one ever will. We harbor all these unnecessarily toxic thoughts in our mind, which only makes it worse than it already is.

Rejection makes us sad, angry, lonely, and depressed. That's the reason no one wants to go through it, because it only ends up bringing lasting negative emotions into our lives, which is no fun at all. After rejection happens, it's hard to take it back. Have you ever heard someone say something bad about you? They say that they didn't mean it that way, but the emotional damage is already done. It's difficult not to believe something or experience its pain once it has already been said.

Rejection hurts because it can lead us to thinking less about ourselves. Our confidence and hope is lost and we tend to think the worst about ourselves. This makes it more difficult to build up our confidence again. We feel lost and broken, and we feel like there's nothing we can do about it.

When we experience rejection, our bodies react physically, too. We can lose our appetite, our body can tremble, we lose motivation for life and struggle to get out of bed, we lie awake for hours thinking of the rejection, and more. Depending on how badly hurt you felt or how bad the situation is, your body will react differently each time. For some, it might get to the point where they can't even get out of bed, while others might only struggle to fall asleep once or twice, and after that they're fine. How your body reacts is unique to each person, but pain is inevitably felt throughout your body and mind.

When rejection and breakups occur, people want an explanation. We're logical and like to think through things clearly. When unexplainable things happen, many have trouble believing it since there's no evidence. When a breakup occurs and there's no logical explanation for it, it leaves us confused and upset.

When I was younger, I went through a tough breakup. The weekend before, me and my partner had an amazing weekend together. I thought everything was perfect. The next weekend he came to my house to break up with me. He tried to give me a reason, but his reasons didn't make sense to me, and I didn't understand why this was happening. In hindsight, I now know that we were never going to work. However, at the time, it left my heart in tatters. I pulled myself back together slowly, but it was hard and upsetting. Unfortunately, not everything makes sense, and that's what makes it even harder.

When a breakup happens, it feels like you're losing a part of yourself. The person you were with was so integrated into your life that it becomes difficult to experience life without them. When you lose this person, it feels like you're losing something you worked hard on and spent a lot of time with. Making a relationship work is hard, and when you lose it, you feel like all that work was for nothing. This can hurt because you spent so much time on something you thought would work out in the end.

But, luckily, there are ways we can get over these rejections and breakups and move forward with life. There are ways to thrive again and live a happy and successful life filled with love.

## Techniques To Move On

Moving on from rejection is challenging, but it's necessary to become happy again and to live your life the way you want to.

One of the most important things when going through a breakup is taking care of yourself. When you break up with someone, it's easy to curl up into a ball and isolate yourself from life and daily responsibilities. When going through this, make sure you spend time to build up your confidence and self-worth again. Do things you love and things you didn't get the chance to do when you were in a relationship. Watch your favorite shows, read the book you've been putting off, spend time pampering yourself, and eat food that you enjoy eating. You should be the number one priority on your list.

Dressing up nicely just because you want to also puts you in a better mood, rather than lying around in sweats and an oversized shirt. Dress up for yourself and wear things you like. Impress yourself and don't try to impress anyone else.

To move on, you can spend time with your friends and family. We often want to punish ourselves because of a breakup, but you're allowed to laugh and have fun. We also often isolate ourselves because we think we'll feel better just wallowing in our own emotions. But sharing our emotions with others can help us feel better. When others try to make us feel better, it can make us feel that at least someone cares. It helps to feel that others still love and care for us.

Don't ignore the emotions you're feeling; suppressing and bottling them up isn't good for your mental health. Tell yourself that it's okay to feel the emotions that you're feeling. If your emotions become too much for you, you can write them down or share them with others. This can help you work through them.

If you want to move on, stop your thoughts from running wild. It does you more damage to think negatively about yourself than to tell yourself that it happened, and you have to move on from it. Don't let the negativity overwhelm your mind. If you think you aren't good enough to receive love, stop these thoughts immediately. Tell yourself that it's nonsense and that you're worthy of receiving love. You're strong and amazing and you can get through this. Remind yourself that there were two of you in the relationship, and it's not only you that should take the blame. Make sure these negative thoughts don't run wild in your head. The only way to move on is to make sure you don't beat yourself up about it.

Don't see the relationship as a waste of time. Every relationship means something and happens for a reason. We have to go through them in order to become stronger. There's always a reason for what happens. Even if your ex helped you realize what you don't want in a partner, that's still a positive outcome.

Think about what you learned throughout the relationship and what you can take away from it. Even if it's the smallest lesson, it's still something. If you think that it was a waste of time, it's just going to make you feel worse about it. Look at it in an optimistic way.

You're allowed to mourn and go through all the emotions

you have to. Grieving is a part of losing something you once had in your life, or missing something you could have had. Accept that you must feel these feelings.

To get over a breakup, you must try to create a new normal for you. Try adapting to this new normal. Human beings can adapt to different situations, even when it sometimes feels difficult. You have to figure out a new routine for yourself. When you're in a relationship, your life is heavily integrated with your partner's. Now you have to learn how to live on your own again. Instead of going to places you and your ex went to together, find new places where you can make new memories. Start changing your life for the better. Try new things and find different things that make you happy. Find joy in other areas of your life.

Moving on from a breakup often means moving on from the person, too. Sometimes it's best to completely remove yourself from this person's life. If you still text and talk to your ex, it's often harder to move on and start anew. It all depends on you and how you're feeling. If you feel you should slowly sever ties, but you can't do it immediately, that's perfectly fine. If, after a while of texting, you realize it's making you feel worse than you already do, make the decision to stop talking to them. Make sure that you're focusing on what you're feeling and how you can feel better.

A good way to start moving on from your previous relationship is by meeting new people. Don't be scared to get back out there and go on dates again. I know doing this all over again can feel tiring and depressing but think about the exciting new possibilities instead. Get yourself out there and have fun. This doesn't mean you have to jump into a new relationship immediately. It's good to feel how it is to be single again first. But just going out and having fun again will make us feel better about the heartache we're feeling.

Now that we've started our journey towards moving on and healing, we must learn how to be happy in the present moment, and how to enjoy and soak in each moment of life.

## How To Be Happy In The Moment

Being happy in the moment is all about thinking of what's going on in your life right now. Forget about the past mistakes and the future worries and focus on the happy present. Notice the small things in your day and appreciate them. Look at where you are in life and how far you have already come. Choose to make the present moment happy. You're alive, you have great things in your life, and you're worthy of happiness. There are multiple ways to be happy in the present moment.

If you're feeling like your days are monotonous, try to do something out of the ordinary. Make a change of scenery and soak in the day. Look at the world around you and get out of your own bubble.

If you're unhappy at the moment, focus on someone else. Talk to people and do kind things for them. If we focus on others, it helps us get out of our own troubles and to forget about all the things we have to do or all the responsibilities we have. It also makes us feel good when we can do things for others.

Live your life the way you want to. If you're doing things you believe shouldn't be a part of your life, then it's time for a change. Think about the values you have and the life you're living and see if they're aligning. If they're not, make changes to live the life you want. This will help you live in the present moment and be happy within it.

To live in the moment, you must let go of the things that

you've

dwelled on for a long time. You must learn to move past them and think of how grateful you are of the life you have now. This will take some time to work through and it is a process, but once you've managed to move past it, your life will become better because of it.

Notice things that people say to you. Because we aren't living in the moment, we often shrug off the nice things that people do for us or the kind compliments they give. When someone gives you a compliment, don't take it for granted. Be happy about the compliment. Don't tell yourself that it isn't genuine, or they don't know what they're talking about. Tell yourself that it's amazing how thoughtful they are.

When something new and exciting happens in your present life, don't hide away or be scared of the experience. Go for it and enjoy it for what it is. Even though you don't know how the experience will turn out, try it anyway. We often shy away from experiences because we're scared of them being negative. However, if we don't join in the experience, we might miss one of the best experiences we ever had. Take the risk rather than ignoring all the fun possibilities you might have.

Being happy for others often helps us to be happy. When you're jealous, it makes you feel upset and like you aren't good enough. When you're genuinely happy for others, it helps to make you feel happy, too. Be proud of what others are achieving, even if you're not achieving it yourself. Make it a point to be happy in the moment.

In this chapter, we've highlighted the following:

- Why rejection hurts
- How we can move on from rejection
- How to be happy in the present moment

Rejection, heartache, and breakups aren't easy. We will never experience the same pain or the same feelings. There are a lot of reasons why they hurt so much, and nobody can tell you that you should get over it already because they've never felt the same heart crushing moment you've felt.

However, taking the first step is a great leap forward. I'm proud of you for making even a little bit of progress. Working your way through these techniques to help you move on will pay off in the end. Take it step by step. Go at your own pace, and don't listen to what others have to say. Once you can get through this pain, you can start to live in the moment and become happy in each moment of your life. This is a lifelong journey, but as long as you keep trying, you will reach where you want to be.

I'm rooting for you, and I know you'll get there in the end. It's a fight, but it's a fight worth fighting.

## Conclusion

Sometimes the heart sees what is invisible to the eye.
- H. Jackson Brown Jr.

# THE LOVE FORMULA

What's the magical love formula you can drink to instantly fall in love and live happily ever after? That love formula can only be found in the best fantasy books. However, we do have the power to create our own magic love formula that can bring us ecstatic joy in the end. It takes a long time to brew and work out the kinks, but as soon as it's complete, you'll be filled with joy and love.

Everyone's journey to love is different. For some it might be love at first sight, while for others it might be going through many heartaches to find the genuine love you're looking for. It doesn't matter what your journey is; the destination will be incredible. And once you've reached this destination, the journey will continue on with your loved one.

The journey of discovering our love formula throughout this book has started with what love really is. It's looked at how there are many meanings people attach to love, and how love is complicated and straightforward at the same time. We've looked at how love affects our bodies and minds, and how it's an abstract feeling with a concrete effect. We've looked at the different types of love, such as eros, philia, and agape, and we've learned why we all crave and need love.

Next, we looked at what love is as opposed to what it isn't. We've looked at how love is lasting, and thus opposite to infatuation, lust, and obsession. We discovered that there can be lust, infatuation, and obsession within love, but they shouldn't overpower or overwhelm. Attraction must turn into love for it to become genuine love, and it's something that's short-lived. We finished off by asking you a question to test if you really are in love. This is something to think about that will help to distinguish true love from attraction.

The next stage of understanding love was to understand your feelings and emotions. We learned why we should set our emotions free and how to do it. Unfortunately, we've also seen that love hurts, but the only way to open yourself up to it is to be vulnerable. I've taught you how to set your emotions free and what good it will do for you.

Next we moved on to the different stages of love. We discovered how love starts with butterflies and hearts in our eyes, and how it moves onto something more serious. We've learned that it's normal to have misunderstandings and difficulties that result in arguments, and that once you've conquered that, there's a deep love and harmony that follows. We've seen that love can grow over time, and that there's a possibility for everlasting love.

In the last chapter of part one, we discovered what finding "The One" means. We figured out if we really need to find "The One" and how we can attract them. We looked at who "The One" really is, and how important it is to love and find yourself. We jumped into the world of self-love and realized what we need to do in order to find a wonderful partner.

Part two was all about giving you tips to succeed in your love life. We started off with general communication and connection skills to help you form bonds with friends, family, acquaintances, and love interests. We described all the love languages and explained how to notice what someone's love language actually is. It's important to know how to create a platonic friendship bond first before you can move into something romantic, and we explored this within this chapter.

The next chapter focused on the most important part; your dating survival guide. It explained all about first dates, how to ask someone out, how to make a move on them, when the perfect moment is for a first kiss, how you can make the kiss memorable, how to ask someone to be official, and how to talk about expectations. There were also first date ideas and tips on how to know what the right moment is to ask someone out on a date.

After talking all about dates and love interests, we moved on to what to do when your love interest has friendzoned you. How can you get out of the friend zone, and what if you can't? We also looked at how to handle a situation where you're falling in love with a friend. How can you tell them, and what do you do if they don't reciprocate those feelings?

Lastly, we focused on what to do if it goes wrong. We looked at rejection and breakups, and how hard they can be to get through. We gave you techniques for moving on and what you can do to become happier in the present moment. Knowing that you're not alone and that you're worthy of love is very important to understand. Things will get better over time and remember that everyone has to go through these things at least once in their lives.

This book isn't meant to tell you what exactly to do to find the perfect love—I don't think anyone can tell you that for sure. But it should give you encouragement and support, and help you understand that you deserve the love that you want. It should reassure you that you will find the right partner for you. It might take a month or a year, but you'll get there. I'm also here to remind you that you don't have to find a partner, and not to let pressure from others get to you. If you want to live without a partner, it's your choice, and there isn't anything wrong with that, either. As long as you're happy in life, that's all that matters.

Stay calm and patient and know that you can and will find love. Use these tips and tricks to help you find that love and be happy within it. Remember that there's no rush to find love; you have your whole life ahead of you!

THE LOVE FORMULA

# Something for you

I wanted to share with you a special gift that I believe can make a positive impact in your life. It's a free self-love and self-improvement affirmation sheet that I've created to help you cultivate a more positive and empowering mindset.

The sheet is filled with uplifting affirmations that you can read and repeat to yourself every day. By focusing on these affirmations, you can train your mind to adopt a more confident and self-assured perspective, and make progress towards becoming the best version of yourself.

I truly believe that self-love and self-improvement are key to a fulfilling life, and I hope that this affirmation sheet can be a helpful tool in your journey. If you'd like to receive your free copy, please just let me know and I'll be happy to send it over.

Wishing you all the best,

*Venus Galena*
**Venus Galena**

SCAN TO GET YOUR
**GIFT!**

*Your daily*
**SELF LOVE**
AFFIRMATIONS

**369**
**AFFIRMATIONS**
to empowering yourself to grow and develop an unbreakable positive mindset

# Thank you

I just wanted to take a moment to thank you for taking the time to read my book. It means so much to me that you gave it a chance and I truly hope you enjoyed it.

If you feel inclined, I would love for you to leave a review or a star rating on Amazon (a rating would only take two clicks). Your thoughts and feedback would mean the world to me and would help other potential readers make a decision about picking up my book.

Thank you again for your support and I can't wait for you to see what's next!

Best,

*Venus Galena*

Venus Galena

Scan codes below to leave your feedback:

US  UK  CA

# Glossary

**Testosterone:** This is the male sex hormone that advances sexual development and functions.

**Estrogen:** This is the female sex hormone that develops sexual and reproductive systems in women.

**Norepinephrine (Noradrenaline):** This is a hormone that helps our bodies respond to emergencies. It's the fight-or-flight response we experience in certain circumstances.

**Phenylethylamine:** This is a chemical that's made within the body and helps to combat depression, boost your mood, and improve your attention span.

**Oxytocin:** This is often called the "love hormone" because it helps with reproduction in the male and female body. In males it helps move sperm, and in females it initiates breast milk and labor.

**Vasopressin:** This is a hormone that controls thermoregulation (controlling body temperature) among other things in the body.

**Attraction:** This is all about drawing someone in. When someone is attracted to you, something draws them toward you. Whether it's physical, emotional, or spiritual, you appeal to them in some way.

# References

A Conscious Rethink. (2020, June 10). *9 Painful Reasons Why Love Hurts So Much*. A Conscious Rethink. https://www.aconsciousrethink.com/13401/why-love-hurts/

Abramson, A. (2021, December 16). *How To Have The Dreaded "What Are We" Convo*. Bustle. https://www.bustle.com/wellness/how-to-make-relationship-official

Alston, T. (2020, August 6). *Why Expressing Emotions Is Beneficial? | Empower Your Mind*. Tracy Alston | Optimize Your Mental Performance. https://tracyalston.com/why-expressing-emotions-is-beneficial/

B, B., & Sadie. (2021, August 23). *Why Do People Need Love in Their Life?* PairedLife - Relationships. https://pairedlife.com/love/Why-Humans-Need-Love#:~:text=We%20use%20love%20to%20drive

BBC Home. (2014, September 17). *BBC Science | Human Body & Mind | Science of Love*. Bbc.co.uk. https://www.bbc.co.uk/science/hottopics/love/

Bhavan, B. V. (n.d.). *True Love According to Socrates (469-399 B.C.)*. Www.speakingtree.in. Retrieved July 4, 2022, from https://www.speakingtree.in/blog/true-love-according-to-socrates-469399-bc

Bockmann, M. (n.d.). *Why Does Love Hurt in a Relationship? 5 Surprising Reasons*. Thriveglobal.com. https://thriveglobal.com/stories/why-does-love-hurt-in-a-relationship-5-surprising-reasons/

Borenstein, J. (2020, February 12). *Self-Love and What It Means*. Brain & Behavior Research Foundation. https://www.bbrfoundation.org/blog/self-love-and-what-it-means#:~:text=It%20means%20accepting%20your%20emotions

Brandon, J. (2014, May 29). *10 Simple Ways to Make People Like You More*. Time. https://time.com/135945/make-people-like-you/

Brown, L. (2020, June 8). *How to tell if someone likes you: 28 surprising signs they're into you!* Hack Spirit. https://hackspirit.com/how-to-tell-if-someone-likes-you-15-surprising-signs-theyre-into-you/

Campo, N., & Engle, G. (2022, June 8). How to Kiss Someone Like You Mean It. *Self*. https://www.self.com/story/best-kissing-advice

Cassata, C. (2021, January 25). *Social Pain: What It Is and 6 Ways to Cope Safely*. Healthline. https://www.healthline.com/health-news/yes-youre-probably-experiencing-social-pain-right-now-how-to-cope

Cleveland Clinic. (n.d.). *Norepinephrine: What It Is, Function, Deficiency & Side Effects*. Cleveland Clinic. https://my.clevelandclinic.org/health/articles/22610-norepinephrine-noradrenaline#:~:text=Norepinephrine%20(Noradrenaline)

Cocchimiglio, S. (n.d.). *How To Last Through The 5 Stages Of Love | Betterhelp*. Www.betterhelp.com. https://www.betterhelp.com/advice/love/how-to-last-through-the-5-stages-of-love/

Coelho, P. (n.d.). *Paulo Coelho on love - Google Search*. Www.google.com. Retrieved June 21, 2022, from https://www.google.com/search?q=Paulo+Coelho+on+love&sxsrf=ALiCzsagRGJqO_B1cEevxsTq8sZ2GkKwHA:1654589551801&source=lnms&tbm=isch&sa=X&ved=2ahUKEwiGwO-z8pr4AhVRXcAKHQjLBvEQ_AUoAXoECAIQAw&biw=1366&bih=625&dpr=1

Colby, S. (2019, December 7). *21 Ways To Live In The*

142

*Moment And Be Happy Right Now.* Happier Human. https://www.happierhuman.com/live-moment/

CSU MarComm Staff. (2017, January 18). *10 ways to connect with your partner daily.* SOURCE. https://source.colostate.edu/10-ways-connect-partner-daily/

Deitz, B. (2015, December 30). *45 Little Ways You Can Tell If Someone Is Into You.* Bustle. https://www.bustle.com/articles/132431-45-little-ways-you-can-tell-if-someone-is-into-you

Eharmony Editorial Team. (2018, January 2). *WHEN'S THE RIGHT TIME FOR A FIRST KISS? 5 WAYS TO TELL IF YOUR DATE IS READY.* https://www.eharmony.com/dating-advice/getting-to-know/5-ways-to-tell-if-your-date-wants-a-kiss/

Engle, G., & Zane, Z. (2020, September 28). *Here's the Right Way to Ask Somebody Out.* Men's Health. https://www.menshealth.com/sex-women/a25413723/how-to-ask-someone-out-date/

Fatherly. (2021, March 25). *30 Small, Nice Ways to Connect with Your Partner.* Fatherly. https://www.fatherly.com/love-money/stay-connected-to-partner-marriage

Faubion, D. (2022, June 17). *Help! You Are Falling In Love With Your Best Friend | BetterHelp.* Www.betterhelp.com. https://www.betterhelp.com/advice/relations/what-to-do-when-youre-falling-in-love-with-a-friend/

Fellizar, K. (2018, October 26). *How To Tell The Difference Between Love And Obsession.* Bustle. https://www.bustle.com/p/how-to-tell-the-difference-between-love-obsession-13000434

Gonsalves, K. (2021, January 22). *Are You In Love — Or Just Infatuated? Here's How To Tell The Difference.* Mindbodygreen. https://www.mindbodygreen.com/articles/is-it-love-or-infatuation-how-to-know-when-youre-infatuated/

Gordon, S. (2020, June 27). *Everything You Need to Know About the Five Love Languages.* Verywell Mind. https://

www.verywellmind.com/can-the-five-love-languages-help-your-relationship-4783538

Gregoire, C. (2014, May 21). *6 Habits Of People In Happy Marriages*. HuffPost. https://www.huffpost.com/entry/psychology-of-lasting-love_n_5339457

Healthline. (2018, August 30). *Is There Really A "Love Hormone"?* Healthline. https://www.healthline.com/health/love-hormone#what-is-it

History.com Editors. (2009, November 9). *Plato*. HISTORY. https://www.history.com/topics/ancient-history/plato#:~:text=The%20Athenian%20philosopher%20Plato%20(c

Hoxha, L. (n.d.). *7 Reasons Why Love is Important for Human Beings*. 7 Reasons Why Love Is Important for Human Beings. Retrieved June 21, 2022, from https://luciahoxha.com/2018/06/7-reasons-why-love-is-important-for-human-beings/

Jacobson, S. (2017, March 21). *Connecting With People - What It Is and Isn't, And Why You Might Find It Hard*. Harley Therapy™ Blog. https://www.harleytherapy.co.uk/counselling/connecting-with-people.htm

Jacobson, S. (2020, June 23). *Why Does Love Hurt? And How to Make it Stop*. Harley Therapy™ Blog. https://www.harleytherapy.co.uk/counselling/why-does-love-hurt.htm

Jafri, M. (2009, October 9). *Does love diminish or grow as time passes?* Daily Sundial. https://sundial.csun.edu/6153/archive/doeslovediminishorgrowastimepasses/#:~:text=Yes%2C%20it%20grows%2C%20and%20it

Johns Hopkins Medicine. (n.d.). *Estrogen's Effects on the Female Body*. Www.hopkinsmedicine.org. https://www.hopkinsmedicine.org/health/conditions-and-diseases/estrogens-effects-on-the-female-body#:~:text=Estrogens%20are%20a%20group%20of

Jowett, B. (n.d.). *Socrates on Love*. Aquestionofexistence.com. Retrieved June 21, 2022, from http://aquestionofexistence.com/Aquestionofexistence/Socrates_on_Love.html

Kabic, J. (2022, March 8). *How to Get Out of the Friend Zone [10 Proven Methods]*. Review42. https://review42.com/uk/resources/how-to-get-out-of-the-friend-zone/

Kale, S. (2019, July 2). *How to tell your best friend you're in love with them – by those who have taken the plunge*. The Guardian. https://www.theguardian.com/lifeandstyle/2019/jul/02/how-to-tell-your-best-friend-youre-in-love-with-them-by-those-who-have-taken-the-plunge

Kane, S. (2019, September 1). *How to Be Honestly Happy in the Present Moment*. Psych Central. https://psychcentral.com/blog/how-to-be-honestly-happy-in-the-present-moment#3

Karantzas, G. (2019). *Will I Ever Find "The One"?* Psychology Today. https://www.psychologytoday.com/us/blog/the-science-love/201905/will-i-ever-find-the-one

Kassel, G. (2021, January 28). *There's a Difference Between Love and Lust — But It Varies*. Healthline. https://www.healthline.com/health/relationships/difference-between-love-and-lust#identify-or-spark-lust

Kate. (2018, April 30). *21 Ways on How to Make Someone Like You*. Luvze. https://www.luvze.com/how-to-make-someone-like-you/

Khoshaba, D. (2012, March 20). *The Early Stages of Falling in Love | Psychology Today*. Www.psychologytoday.com. https://www.psychologytoday.com/us/blog/get-hardy/201203/the-early-stages-falling-in-love#:~:text=Key%20points

King, S. L. (2021, May 17). *Think You're Falling in Love? Here's What Science Says*. Oprah Daily. https://www.oprahdaily.com/life/relationships-love/a29267937/how-to-know-falling-in-love/

Konstan, D. (2008). ARISTOTLE ON LOVE AND FRIENDSHIP. *Aristotle on Love and Friendship, 2*(2). https://classics.nsu.ru/schole/2/2-2-konstan.pdf

Laderer, A. (2018, November 13). *Why Rejection Hurts (and 3 Ways to Dust Yourself Off)*. Talkspace. https://www.talkspace.com/blog/why-rejection-hurts/

Laderer, A., & Mcknight, J. (2022, January 20). *How your brain changes when you fall in love and 4 health benefits*. Insider. https://www.insider.com/guides/health/sex-relationships/what-is-love

Lamothe, C. (2019, October 29). *Lack of Communication: 17 Tips for Couples*. Healthline. https://www.healthline.com/health/lack-of-communication#communication-tips

Lawson, K. (2017, February 14). *Why Loving Someone Can Hurt So Much*. Www.vice.com. https://www.vice.com/en/article/paepyz/why-loving-someone-can-hurt-so-much

Lebowitz, S. (2020, October 19). *15 psychological tricks to make people like you immediately*. The Independent. https://www.independent.co.uk/life-style/sixteen-psychological-tricks-people-like-you-a7967861.html

Livingstone-Peters, S. (2020, February 14). *The science of love*. International Science Council. https://council.science/current/blog/the-science-of-love/

Lonczak, H. S. (2020, December 24). *How to Express Your Emotions in A Healthy Way: 30 Practical Tips*. PositivePsychology.com. https://positivepsychology.com/express-emotions/

Longman, M. (2019, June 7). *Should You Tell Your Best Friend You're In Love With Them?* Www.refinery29.com. https://www.refinery29.com/en-us/in-love-with-best-friend-what-to-do

Low, S. (2018, January 18). *The Science Behind Why We Fall in Love*. Mount Elizabeth Hospital. https://

www.mountelizabeth.com.sg/healthplus/article/the-science-behind-why-we-fall-in-love#:~:text=The%20initial%20happy%20feelings%20of

Lusinski, N. (2018, April 11). *9 Ways To Attract "The One" Into Your Life, According To Religious Leaders*. Bustle. https://www.bustle.com/p/9-ways-to-attract-the-one-into-your-life-according-to-religious-leaders-8756328

Martin, R. (2018, March 1). *10 Perfect Questions to Ask On The First Date To Really Get To Know Someone*. One Love Foundation. https://www.joinonelove.org/learn/10-perfect-questions-to-ask-on-the-first-date-to-really-get-to-know-someone/

Martin, S. (2018, February 10). *How to Love Yourself: 22 Simple Ideas*. Live Well with Sharon Martin. https://www.livewellwithsharonmartin.com/how-to-love-yourself/

MasterClass Staff. (2020, November 8). *Effective Communication: 6 Ways to Improve Communication Skills*. https://www.masterclass.com/articles/how-to-improve-your-communication-skills#quiz-0

Mirriam-Webster.com. (n.d.). *Definition of ATTRACTION*. Www.merriam-Webster.com. https://www.merriam-webster.com/dictionary/attraction

Mitrokostas, S. (2019, February 14). *Why breakups hurt mentally, emotionally, and physically - Insider*. Insider; Insider. https://www.insider.com/why-do-breakups-hurt-so-much-2019-2

Mody, N. (2019, May 28). *Do We Need to Find "The One"?* Ascent Publication. https://medium.com/the-ascent/do-we-need-to-find-the-one-5a363cd339ca

Mosely, A. (n.d.). *Philosophy of Love | Internet Encyclopedia of Philosophy*. Internet Encyclopedia of Philosophy. https://iep.utm.edu/love/#H3

Naim, R. (2016, February 10). *30 Ways You Can Tell The Difference Between Love And Infatuation*. Thought Catalog.

https://thoughtcatalog.com/rania-naim/2016/02/30-ways-you-can-tell-the-difference-between-love-and-infatuation/

Nast, C., & McCracken, A. (2022, March 4). *How to (Actually) Love Yourself, According to Experts.* SELF. https://www.self.com/story/how-to-love-yourself

News@AUC. (n.d.). *Top Three Reasons Why We Fall in Love | The American University in Cairo.* Www.aucegypt.edu. https://www.aucegypt.edu/news/stories/top-three-reasons-why-we-fall-love

Nguyen, E. (n.d.). *15 Habits That Will Help You Attract The Right Partner Into Your Life.* Loveful Mind. https://lovefulmind.com/posts/15-habits-help-you-attract-the-right-partner-into-your-life

Ospino, L. (2021, November 24). Platonic Love: The Concept of the Greek Philosopher Plato. *Greek Reporter.* https://greekreporter.com/2021/11/24/platonic-love-concept-greek-philosopher-plato/

Owsley, D. (2018, July 20). *21 Ways to Communicate Effectively.* Relavate. https://www.relavate.org/communicate-well/2018/7/20/21-ways-to-communicate-effectively

Pai, R. (2021, May 5). *Love Vs Obsession: 20 Main Differences.* MomJunction. https://www.momjunction.com/articles/love-vs-obsession-differences_00725888/

Patel, D. (2019, May 15). *14 Proven Ways to Improve Your Communication Skills.* Entrepreneur. https://www.entrepreneur.com/article/300466

Petsinger, K. (2015, November 13). *8 Insanely Effective Ways To Connect With Anyone You Meet.* Lifehack. https://www.lifehack.org/332706/8-insanely-effective-ways-connect-with-anyone-you-meet

Prabhat, S. (2010, February 8). *Difference Between Love and Obsession | Difference Between.* Difference between Love and Obsession. http://www.differencebetween.net/

miscellaneous/difference-between-love-and-obsession/#:~:text=Love%20is%20a%20feeling%20from

Raghunathan, R. (2014, January 8). *The Need to Love*. Psychology Today. https://www.psychologytoday.com/us/blog/sapient-nature/201401/the-need-love

Ramsdale, S. (2008, December 18). *True love really does last forever – we've got the proof*. Marie Claire. https://www.marieclaire.co.uk/news/true-love-really-does-last-forever-173959

Raylin says. (2015, August 10). *Falling In Love with Your Best Friend - What to Do?* TheHopeLine.com. https://www.thehopeline.com/51-falling-in-love-with-your-best-friend/

Raypole, C. (2020a, July 30). *Hey You! Quit Hiding Your Feelings*. Healthline. https://www.healthline.com/health/mental-health/hiding-feelings#why-its-done

Raypole, C. (2020b, August 5). *15 Effects of Love on Your Brain and Body*. Healthline. https://www.healthline.com/health/relationships/effects-of-love#brain-effects

Raypole, C. (2022, May 18). *Here's How to Tell If You Love Someone — and What to Do*. Healthline. https://www.healthline.com/health/relationships/how-do-you-know-you-love-someone#signs-to-watch-for

Regier, M. W. (2021, February 2). *What Love Truly Means, According To A Therapist*. YourTango. https://www.yourtango.com/experts/michael-regier/what-is-love

Relationships. (2020, November 10). *The No-Bullshit Way to Find "The One."* Mark Manson. https://markmanson.net/how-to-find-the-one

Rhodes, S. (2017, November 15). *Why We Have a Need for Affection*. EverydayHealth.com. https://www.everydayhealth.com/healthy-living/why-we-have-need-affection/

Scribner, H. (2015, June 15). *10 things you need to know about finding The One*. Deseret News. https://www.deseret.com/2015/6/15/20566700/10-things-you-need-to-know-about-finding-the-one

Seltzer, L. F. (2011, September 28). *Why We Hide Emotional Pain | Psychology Today South Africa*. Www.psychologytoday.com. https://www.psychologytoday.com/za/blog/evolution-the-self/201109/why-we-hide-emotional-pain

Sharman, A., & Low, J. (2008). Vasopressin and its role in critical care. *Continuing Education in Anaesthesia Critical Care & Pain*, 8(4), 134–137. https://doi.org/10.1093/bjaceaccp/mkn021

Smith, S. (2021, July 20). *15 Signs Someone Is Hiding Their Feelings for You*. Marriage Advice - Expert Marriage Tips & Advice. https://www.marriage.com/advice/relationship/signs-someone-is-hiding-their-feelings-for-you/

*Socrates' View Of Love - 1035 Words | 123 Help Me*. (n.d.). Www.123helpme.com. https://www.123helpme.com/essay/Socrates-View-Of-Love-81356

Soekn-Huberty, E. (2021, April 17). *10 Reasons Why Self-Love Is Important*. The Important Site. https://theimportantsite.com/10-reasons-why-self-love-is-important/

Taylor, J., Engle, G., & Polk, M. (2022, May 24). *52 First Date Ideas That Will Help You Land a Second One*. Men's Health. https://www.menshealth.com/sex-women/a19517930/best-first-date-ideas/

The Angry Therapist. (2018, February 17). *You have to love yourself before you can love someone else — is bullshit*. Medium. https://angrytherapist.medium.com/you-have-to-love-yourself-before-you-can-love-someone-else-is-bullshit-2a43e59cffe3

The Animated Woman. (2020, March 23). *18 Ways To Get Out Of The Friendzone – Brilliant Tips That Actually Work*. Bonobology.com. https://www.bonobology.com/ways-get-out-friendzone/

The Jed Foundation. (n.d.). *The Painful Truth About Breakups / JED*. The Jed Foundation. Retrieved June 21, 2022, from https://jedfoundation.org/resource/the-painful-truth-about-breakups/#:~:text=Initiating%20a%20breakup%20when%20the

The School of Life. (n.d.). *Why True Love Doesn't Have to Last Forever - The School Of Life*. Www.theschooloflife.com. Retrieved June 21, 2022, from https://www.theschooloflife.com/article/why-true-love-doesnt-have-to-last-forever/

*The Symposium: 201d - 204c*. (n.d.). SparkNotes. https://www.sparknotes.com/philosophy/symposium/section9/

The University of Kansas Health System. (n.d.). *Why is Emotional Expression Important?* Www.kansashealthsystem.com. https://www.kansashealthsystem.com/health-resources/turning-point/programs/resilience-toolbox/emotional-expression/why-is-emotional-expression-important#:~:text=Just%20by%20doing%20that%2C%20we

Thorp, T. (2017, March 2). *The Chopra Center*. The Chopra Center. https://chopra.com/articles/10-ways-to-deepen-your-connections-with-others

Torrisi, L. T., Rosara. (2021, January 27). *How to tell the difference between lust and love, according to relationship experts*. Insider. https://www.insider.com/guides/health/mental-health/lust-vs-love

Uniacke, K. (2018, September 1). *How to tell someone you like them (and NOT ruin the friendship)*. A Conscious Rethink. https://www.aconsciousrethink.com/8573/tell-someone-you-like-them/

Urology Care Foundation. (n.d.). *Low Testosterone: Symptoms, Diagnosis & Treatment - Urology Care Foundation*. Www.urologyhealth.org. https://www.urologyhealth.org/

urology-a-z/l/low-testosterone#:~:text=Testosterone%20is
%20the%20male%20sex

Van Edwards, V. (2021, September 7). *How to Get Out of The Friend Zone in 4 Steps (With Science!)*. Science of People. https://www.scienceofpeople.com/friendzone/

Vanessa Van Edwards. (2016, June 9). *How to Ask Someone...* Science of People; Science of People. https://www.scienceofpeople.com/how-to-ask-someone-out/

Walton, A. G. (2018, January 24). *7 Ways To Become A Little Happier In The Moment*. Forbes. https://www.forbes.com/sites/alicegwalton/2018/01/24/7-ways-to-become-just-a-little-happier-in-the-moment/?sh=11563af4770c

WebMD. (n.d.). *PHENETHYLAMINE (PEA): Overview, Uses, Side Effects, Precautions, Interactions, Dosing and Reviews*. Www.webmd.com. Retrieved June 21, 2022, from https://www.webmd.com/vitamins/ai/ingredientmono-1274/phenethylamine-pea#:~:text=Phenethylamine%20stimulates%20the%20body%20to

*What is the science of love? | The Anatomy Of Love*. (2016). The Anatomy of Love. https://theanatomyoflove.com/faq/what-is-the-science-of-love/

Widmer, B. (2016, November 7). *Why Rejection Hurts So Bad - And How To Overcome The Pain*. Lifehack. https://www.lifehack.org/490129/why-rejection-hurts-so-bad-and-how-to-overcome-the-pain

Winch, G. (2013, July 3). *10 Surprising Facts About Rejection | Psychology Today South Africa*. Www.psychologytoday.com. https://www.psychologytoday.com/za/blog/the-squeaky-wheel/201307/10-surprising-facts-about-rejection#:~:text=Rejection%20piggybacks%20on%20physical%20pain

Zane, Z. (2021, May 3). *Smart People Always Ask These Questions on a First Date*. Men's Health. https://www.menshealth.com/sex-women/a30979320/first-date-questions/

# Image References

Alleksana. (2021). Gifts on Red Surface [Image]. In *Pexels*. https://www.pexels.com/photo/gifts-on-red-surface-6478864/

Bazzocco, M. (2019). Self love Sunday. Bath salts, vegan chocolate, tea and a book [Image]. In *Unsplash*. https://unsplash.com/photos/TOZqUHD8L38

Belle Co. (2018). Silhouette Photography of Group of People Jumping during Golden Time [Image]. In *Pexels*. https://www.pexels.com/photo/silhouette-photography-of-group-of-people-jumping-during-golden-time-1000445/

Cottonbro. (2020). Person Holding White Printer Paper [Image]. In *Pexels*. https://www.pexels.com/photo/person-holding-white-printer-paper-3826670/

Cottonbro. (2021). Photo of an Elderly Couple Sitting on a Wooden Bench [Image]. In *Pexels*. https://www.pexels.com/photo/photo-of-an-elderly-couple-sitting-on-a-wooden-bench-7236496/

Danilyuk, P. (2021). Sitting Blur Reflection Face [Image]. In *Pexels*. https://www.pexels.com/photo/sitting-blur-reflection-face-6417918/

Fewings, N. (2018). Red Heart and Man Drawing Photo [Image]. In *Unsplash*. https://unsplash.com/photos/ka7REB1AJl4

Foster, T. (2018). Man Sitting Beside Woman Also Sitting Outside Photo [Image]. In *Unsplash*. https://unsplash.com/photos/hRZ5s-IPCWE

Hobo, S. (2021). White and Black Heart Drawing Photo [Image]. In *Unsplash*. https://unsplash.com/photos/ZHFk9EeJ7hE

Hughes, E. (2018). Two Women Sitting on White Bench [Image]. In *Pexels*. https://www.pexels.com/photo/two-women-sitting-on-white-bench-1549280/

Lopes, H. (2018). Photograph of Men Having Conversation Seating on Chair [Image]. In *Pexels*. https://www.pexels.com/photo/photograph-of-men-having-conversation-seating-on-chair-1015568/

Mont, U. (2020). Romantic black gays with coffee on street [Image]. In *Pexels*. https://www.pexels.com/photo/romantic-black-gays-with-coffee-on-street-6315331/

Morillo, C. (2018). Two Women Sitting on Chairs Beside Window [Image]. In *Pexels*. https://www.pexels.com/photo/two-women-sitting-on-chairs-beside-window-1181719/

Natalie. (2018). Couple Holding Hands With Red Heart Balloon [Image]. In *Pexels*. https://www.pexels.com/photo/couple-holding-hands-with-red-heart-balloon-1445903/

Pixabay. (2017a). Kid hiding on Pillows [Image]. In *Pexels*. https://www.pexels.com/photo/kid-hiding-on-pillows-262103/

Pixabay. (2017b). Woman Wearing White, Pink, and Green Floral Dress Holding Pink Bougainvillea Flowers [Image]. In *Pexels*. https://www.pexels.com/photo/adult-attractive-beautiful-brunette-206557/

Quốc, D. T. (2017). Red Rose Flower Photo in Dark Surface [Image]. In *Unsplash*. https://unsplash.com/photos/_FSA44MuXn4

Sikkema, K. (2018). Broken Heart Hanging on Wire Photo [Image]. In *Unsplash*. https://unsplash.com/photos/E8H76nY1v6Q

Sklyar, A. (2019). Silhouette of Couple Photo [Image]. In *Unsplash*. https://unsplash.com/photos/-1qIRIqN14A

Wellington, J. (2017). Silhouette Photo of Woman Against during Golden Hour [Image]. In *Pexels*. https://www.pexels.com/photo/silhouette-photo-of-woman-against-during-golden-hour-39853/

Made in the USA
Middletown, DE
22 March 2024